BE REAL IN A

THE BEAUTIFUL TRUTH

A POETRY ODYSSEY

Edited By Lynsey Evans

First published in Great Britain in 2025 by:

Young Writers
Remus House
Coltsfoot Drive
Peterborough
PE2 9BF
Telephone: 01733 890066
Website: www.youngwriters.co.uk

Book Design by Ashley Janson

Softback ISBN 978-1-83685-227-8
Printed and bound in the UK by BookPrintingUK
Website: www.bookprintinguk.com
YB0628E

Foreword

Since 1991, here at Young Writers we have celebrated the awesome power of creative writing, especially in young adults where it can serve as a vital method of expressing their emotions and views about the world around them. In every poem we see the effort and thought that each student published in this book has put into their work and by creating this anthology we hope to encourage them further with the ultimate goal of sparking a life-long love of writing.

Our latest competition for secondary school students, The Beautiful Truth, asked young writers to consider what their truth is, what's important to them, and how to express that using the power of words. We wanted to give them a voice, the chance to express themselves freely and honestly, something which is so important for these young adults to feel confident and listened to. They could give an opinion, highlight an issue, consider a dilemma, impart advice or simply write about something they love. There were no restrictions on style or subject so you will find an anthology brimming with a variety of poetic styles and topics. We hope you find it as absorbing as we have.

We encourage young writers to express themselves and address subjects that matter to them, which sometimes means writing about sensitive or contentious topics. If you have been affected by any issues raised in this book, details on where to find help can be found at **www.youngwriters.co.uk/info/other/contact-lines**

Contents

FREEDOM
BELIEVE!
THE POEMS
HONESTY
TRUTH

I Am Not Ashamed

I am not ashamed,
I am not ashamed that I feel anxious,
I am not ashamed that I struggle,
I am not ashamed that I have only a few close friends,
I am not ashamed that I need extra support,
I am not ashamed that I had to change schools,
I am not ashamed that I have to take medication,
I am not ashamed that I'm not as independent as some,
I am not ashamed that I am picky with foods,
I am not ashamed that I find communication challenging,
I am not ashamed that I won't look you in the eye,
I am not ashamed I use ear defenders to cope with the deafening noise,
I am not ashamed of my sunflower lanyard.

Together, let's make my hidden disability less hidden,
I am not ashamed to be me,
I am not ashamed to be autistic.

Emily Steedman (14)
Basil Paterson Middle School, Edinburgh

Media's Mutation

I am a woman before I am an animal,
I was taught they couldn't be interchangeable,
Taught a skinless face was better than a wrinkle,
My bestial body is inescapable, my anatomy sculpted,
Embellished, plated in gold,
More digestible to the scars and stripes that line my back,
Hair that shields my skin,
Fangs to tear flesh,
The unfeminine natural,
I am nature before I am a woman,
My soul outweighs this body,
Trapped in a vessel of mediocrity and agony,
An incomprehensible identity,
Born from crushed stars and vanity,
Veins like leaves,
Fjords of emotions,
Forests of memories,
Roots spiral around my spine,
Born in a reservoir yet longing for rivers,
Stardust's muse, their fabrication,
Universes concealed behind my mascara-stained eyes,
Shooting stars burn my cheek,
My skin swirls like bark,
My bones mimic their branches,
The laurel tree pleats around me,
Immortals envy me, Papatuanuku cradles me,

Mother Nature's daughter,
Atoms' formation,
She is a girl before she is nature,
She lies motionless as if she too is coated in gold,
Nature cannot nurture her, and every tree has fallen with her,
Roots torn from beneath her,
Roses won't blossom from her fingertips,
Instead, thorns will scale her,
The briar shields her from man's touch,
Collapsed on the soil that bore her,
A braid adorned with marigolds, the only sign a mother once loved her,
No wrinkles kiss her skin,
Silver hair will not trail through her fingers,
She'll be demonised and despised,
Yet they'll eventually celebrate her,
Disguise her savaged body in lilies,
She encapsulates beauty,
Her skin was scarred but young,
Her hair was torn but dark,
Her body was malnourished but slender,
They'll praise her innocence but profit from desire,
What is worse than dying as a little girl?
You could grow old and wither.

Lily Barrass (14)
Basil Paterson Middle School, Edinburgh

Badger

This is my Grampy
My normal poems rhyme and play tricks upon the tongue but for him this cannot be done. The words I wish to use surpass the boundaries of these rules and for this reason I will break my habits and chains as this man deserves the finest ones.

My Grampy was a gardener.
This was his pride and joy.
His garden was his heart, body, and soul.
And to that extent, this garden is my gramps.
Endless hours poured into it smiling away at the bees and butterflies with the birdhouse I bought for him quite a few years ago now.
However, all this work wasn't work to him.
This was his joy, his pride, his happiness.
Grampy was often known as Badger to close friends and family.
I don't know how this name came about but, I can say for certain that it fits.
Badgers play in the dirt and love the outdoors but they're also social and extremely friendly with family and close ones just like my gramps.
Most people didn't see Gramp deteriorate.
But I did.
I'll admit I wasn't always there as I was never the strong one in this family.
If I had to pick out someone in particular, I'd pick out my nan.

My nan is always with my gramp no matter where the two may be.
My nan always goes to see him.
I can't do that.
It hurts too much.
I'd also point out my mom and my stepdad.
To my nan, those two people are like guiding lights which shine upon her engrossing night.
And I will say it shattered me and my family however we struggled through and will continue this.

All I can say is that my Grampy was the life of the party and always will be.
My Grampy was a family man and will forever remain so, but most of all, my Grampy is loved and that alone will never change.

Ty De Bruyn (16)
Bilton School, Bilton

The Beautiful Truth

In the silence of dawn's embrace,
Where the beautiful truth finds its place,
Whispers of wisdom softly trace,
Guiding hearts with gentle grace.

Underneath the starlight sky,
The truth unfolds; no need to pry,
Each moment a chance to clarify,
The beauty that never needs to say goodbye.

In the depths of our soul's sight,
Lies the truth pure and bright,
A beacon in the darkest night,
Guiding us with its eternal light.

As the sun paints the horizon with hues,
Truth reveals itself in the morning's muse,
Each ray - a revelation, no time to lose,
Embracing the beauty, no room for confusion or excuse.

Through the valleys of uncertainty, we tread,
The truth stands steadfast, no fear or dread,
In its presence, all worries are gently shed,
A tapestry of beauty, where souls are lovingly led.

In the whispers of night, secrets unfold,
Truth's melody - timeless and bold,
In every story, in every tale told,
The essence of wisdom - a treasure to behold.

As the moonlight weaves its mystical thread,
Truth's presence, a soothing balm to be spread,
In every moment, in every word said,
The beauty of understanding, where hearts are led.

Beneath the canopy of stars that brightly gleam,
Truth's symphony plays like a timeless dream,
In the river of knowledge, a boundless stream,
Where seekers find solace, where hearts redeem.

Through the tapestry of life's intricate design,
Truth's golden thread weaves, pure and divine,
In the silence of the soul, a sacred shrine,
Where seekers of wisdom eternally align.

Oluwafikemi Olanrewaju (12)
Bilton School, Bilton

The Beautiful Truth

As you explore about, and take massive steps forward, you can see something gazing back at you.
It illuminates like the moon, but is different like doom.
It may be beautiful on the outside but, at times, opposite on the inside.
It's practically air, vanishing clear to the point it's not visible.
Sometimes refreshing and sometimes otherwise.
Fair?
At times you seek it, and at times you conceal from it.
It is just like a mystery.
Your desire is to discover it, but then you are oblivious at times.
It can be a shard, presenting it to be hard.
But in addition, it is sweet, making it a treat,
And sometimes you have to pretend, like a position or role in a play.
You just have to uncover it, like the identity behind the mask.
Puzzles can be compared.
You have to find the astray piece and match it with the destined area.
We may want to reverse it like in a game.
It feels eccentric.
It is fascinating.
Just like this poem, you have to find out what it is that is written behind the lines, and here it is... the beautiful truth.

Bhavika Pavuluri (11)
Bilton School, Bilton

Swimmers In Space

There are a lot unlike us,
Lost in space with planets and dust,
We all hoped the best for them,
After all, they were exploring our milky gem.

They thought they were going to succeed,
Only some managed to get back to their seed,
All our hopes instantly died,
All their loved ones really cried.

We thought they would be remembered forever,
We have thought indeed,
But we've been a lot less clever,
And we forgot their helpful deeds.

They have sacrificed a lot for us,
With hardly any fuss,
Their unstoppable race,
Gave them the name, swimmers in space.

Tapasya Kalahasti (12)
Bilton School, Bilton

The Truth

The truth may be blind if you don't open your eyes and see.
The world in a brighter side, that's the truth.
Society hates the truth, treats it like an outcast.
What did the truth do by simply opening your eyes?
Online when you are laughing, others are crying by sheep wearing a wolf mask.
They don't care, nobody knows who they are.
This is the truth.
Wars, genocide happening everywhere.
They hide this for you to see the fake world this is.
The truth, the happy side is when you don't lie, you will feel better and not guilty.
The truth is the good guy, not bad.

Binta Jaiteh (13)
Bilton School, Bilton

The Beautiful Truth

In a world of filters, facades display,
A longing for authenticity finds its way.
Behind the scenes, where hearts truly lie,
A beauty shines, a truth to spy.

Be real, they say, let your spirit soar,
Embrace the flaws and ask for more.
For in the depths, where honesty resides,
A radiant soul, truly dignified.

The fake world's glamour, a fleeting sight,
Can't match the warmth of genuine light.
So let's cast off the masks, the pretence's art,
And celebrate the beauty of a pure heart.

Sanjana Pradeep (12)
Bilton School, Bilton

The Beautiful Truth

My best friend slowly drifted away
The friend I thought was most
Likely to stay.

She was the friend I thought
Of as us growing up together
And I don't think I could ever
Forget her.

She was the friend I thought would
Dance in the rain with me
I never thought she was the type to
Flee.

She was the friend I thought
Would make jokes and laugh at the
Back of the class with
And now I just sit and watch
Time pass.

She was my friend
I thought.

Ava Ward (12)
Bilton School, Bilton

The Beautiful Truth

I got the text message one night
He said, 'I don't mean to cause a fright
But I don't love you no more
I love your best friend from before'

I begged and begged for him to stay
But he was already on his way
I was left with nothing to spare
Not a single tear left to share

So I sat in bed with a bowl of ice cream
My thoughts sank as deep as a bream
Sat in bed with tissues, all alone
I was no longer in his zone.

Evelyn Hayward-Bradley (11)
Bilton School, Bilton

They Are (Not) An Artist

Hunched over a desk
Digital stylus in their hand
Cramps fill their joints
After 5 hours of work
Re-doing and re-doing until they love it
They are finished
It's not perfect but it's beautiful
They are an artist

Sitting by a canvas
Paint dripping from their brush
They're a mess of paint
After many hours of stiff legs
Painting over and over
They are finished
It's not perfect but it's theirs
They are an artist

Sat by the potter's wheel
Hands stained from the earth's clay
Their back stiff from their terrible posture
After many failed attempts
They finally have the perfect gift for their mum
It's not perfect but it's made with love
They are an artist

Sitting by their computer
Their hands on the keyboard
They've just generated an image
It's only been 30 seconds
No effort to create
It's supposedly perfect but nobody worked hard
They are not an artist

A computer will never replace us
A computer cannot replicate human's work
Our hours of work
Over our desks
Over our sketchbooks
Over our canvas
Over the work we put in
A computer can look perfect
But it has no depth
No love
No beauty
No love

AI will never replace us
AI is not an artist
AI is not art
AI cannot express true emotions
AI cannot capture the truth

It's not art
It's an imitation
It's never the real thing

We are artists
You cannot replace us.

Isabella Packard (13)
Bishop Ramsey CE School, London Borough Of Hillingdon

SOS

So, you live in this world, but do you really care
About all the litter being dropped everywhere?
You tut when you see photos or hear it on the news,
But think about the animals - put yourself in their shoes!
They are losing their homes and their families too,
They need help, but what do you do?
You buy snakeskin shoes for extra swag,
And when you go to the shops you buy a plastic bag!

Our planet is dying, but do you really care?
You still use palm oil products in your hair!
For goodness sake, make an effort, please!
For every second, we are killing more trees!
Think of the orangutans, and the sloths too,
The only ones who can help them are me and you!
So please don't turn away, or pretend you can't hear,
Help before it's too late - they could be extinct next year!

Saying you'll try just isn't enough,
Saving the planet is really tough!
I need all the help I can get,
For our planet is in debt,
For the countless animals we have lost,
And they all come at a terrible cost.
I can say no more, and say no less,
All I can say is SOS!

Molly Cooper (11)
Bishop Ramsey CE School, London Borough Of Hillingdon

Change And Embrace

Though I am young, I can change,
My upbringing and the places I call home,
Roads that stretch from the bustling city roads,
Eventually fade into the tranquillity of the countryside.
I can change and welcome a shift,
A commitment to becoming more,
Carrying lessons carved in my bones,
The echoes of discipline shape my steps.

Though I am underestimated, I can change
Each version of myself,
A reflection of good times and bad -
The strength in vulnerability,
The sadness in laughter,
The confidence which eventually falters.
We must be careful,
We must avoid the barriers that block our way,
Changing and embracing,

Though I'm not fully grown, I can change,
Mature and allow my branches to lengthen,
The green leaves of creativity and innovation,
Acknowledging the rain pouring,
Choosing to ignore,
Limiting the breeze throwing me off my path,
Choosing the sun, the most powerful,
Revealing the warmth of youth once lost.

Though I am still fixing myself, I can change,
Think if we were buildings,
We wouldn't destroy the main foundation,
But instead, renovate,
Replacing what no longer serves us,
With new structures learnt with existence,
Creating spaces where light can flow,
Where change is a celebration,
Not a loss.

Macey Johnson (15)
Bishop Ramsey CE School, London Borough Of Hillingdon

Resilient Reflections!

In shadows where our worries lie
We face the truth, we don't deny
Life's not a fairy tale, we know
But there's strength in every blow
Through sleepless nights and endless thoughts
In battles fought and battles lost
We find a spark, a guiding light
That helps us rise after the fight
A mind's maze, a winding road
With burdens that can overload
Yet in our hearts, a truth does stay
Strength grows stronger every day
In the storm, a beacon glows
Even when the cold wind blows
Each step is hard, each tear is real
But through it all, we start to heal
We honour scars, each story told
Of courage when the nights were cold
In our struggle, we find proof
In rawness, there's a beautiful truth
Behind each mask, a soul fights on
With resilience to greet the dawn
Each moment still, each deep breath taken
Is a sign of hearts unshaken
With heavy days, we find our ways
To navigate through life's tough maze

For every pain, a lesson learned
In fires of life, strength is earned
So we stand tall, not just in fight
But in every quiet, peaceful night
In every heart, the truth will ring
Resilience makes the spirit sing
And in the end, as we pull through
We find within a beautiful truth.

Tara Moore (15)
Bishop Ramsey CE School, London Borough Of Hillingdon

The Beautiful Truth

In the quiet hours of dawn's embrace
My heart whispers softly through time and space
A daughter's love for her mother, pure and true
A bond that shines like morning dew

With every sunrise, I rise to meet her gaze
In her eyes, a universe ablaze
Her strength and grace, an unwavering light
Guiding me through life's darkest night

Through laughter and tears, she stands by my side
A constant presence, a source of pride
Her wisdom flows like a gentle stream
Nurturing my dreams, igniting my dream

In her warmth, I find solace and peace
A sanctuary where my soul can release
The worries of the world, the burdens we bear
She holds them close, with tender care

Her love, a melody that sings in my heart
A symphony of compassion, never to depart
In her arms, I find refuge and rest
A haven where my spirit finds its nest

With each passing day, our bond grows stronger
A tapestry woven, thread by golden thread
A testament to love, unyielding and true
A legacy that will forever renew

So here's to my mother, my guiding star
A beacon of hope, no matter how far
May her love continue to guide my way
As I journey forth, come what may.

Chelsea Nimaro (11)
Bishop Ramsey CE School, London Borough Of Hillingdon

Beach Day

Hear the howling breeze,
Hear the rustling trees,
Hear the shifting sand,
And think, *the beach is so grand.*

See the scuttling crabs,
See the picnic up for grabs,
See the deep, blue bay,
And think, *what a lovely day.*

Feel the spray from the waves,
Feel the wind blow on your face,
Feel the warmth of sunshine rays,
And think of trying to beat friends in a race.

Smell the stench of wet seaweed,
Smell the delicious fresh fish,
Smell the tasty potato chips,
And think, *wouldn't that make a scrumptious dish?*

Taste your vanilla ice cream,
Taste your crispy waffle cone,
Taste the salt from the sea spray,
And think, *is this all a dream?*

Pick up white shells,
And hear distant church bells,
Admire each shell as it shimmers,
Just like the sea when it glimmers.

And when the day is done,
Watching the sunset colours merge into one,
Feel the waves make you wet,
And think, *this is the best beach day yet!*

Anna Mead (11)
Bishop Ramsey CE School, London Borough Of Hillingdon

My Family Tree Of What I Can See

My cousins
My family tree is seeking what I can see
A huge family is not what it seems, why don't you do some maths
I, you, me, we all lose count, 1, 2, 3... *What!*
More than three is great but is too much in a huge family tree
How many?
12 cousins are enough for me but maybe not for you
Be in my shoes, what were you going to do?
Get this straight, this is just my family tree!
All I have for you is men and women jumping from me to you and back to me
We are inseparable, this is just my family tree!

My sister
All I set my heart on is the one I have
She is young and brave and always has my back even if I am the older one
Let us play a game, can you guess who it is?
My heart sinks into fire to have my brown eyes seeing her in despair
Look at her, she is my sister!

My mum and dad
Love of lives and souls are pain that never seems to go away
The tenderness and spirit are never separated
The love of my life is the length of going through every planet and country
And back here to be at my foot.

Yuliana Abdelsayed (11)
Bishop Ramsey CE School, London Borough Of Hillingdon

The Beautiful Truth

The beautiful truth is life,
The cycle of the seasons,
The earth, the people, the feelings.

We all drift,
On the waves of changing times,
All finding our purpose for our lives,
Between these changes,
Time goes round,
With endless meetings and farewells,
It's an eternal cycle,
With more stories to tell.

We are all different,
Different stories and different hearts,
They are not insufficient,
As they are beautiful as they are,
We may be different,
But we've all struggled,
And we've all been happy,
As we have these similarities,
We should embrace each other with love and kindness.

We all have memories,
That have been engraved in our souls,
The people who have made us find ourselves,
The people who have loved us for ourselves.
The people that have formed us into the people we are today.

The beautiful truth is life,
With all its bumps and edges,
It may not be perfect,
But we must love and respect it.

Iris Butler (17)

Bishop Ramsey CE School, London Borough Of Hillingdon

Pressure

School, home, peer:
Wherever you are,
Pressure is near.
Homework, expectations and fitting in
Pushing down on your heart.
Nowhere to begin.

When the end feels near,
Friends seem lost
And your brain is working like a rusty gear
No one is there for you.
At least it feels like
Being last in help's queue

Everyone goes through things:
Bullying, anxiety, trouble
Like being puppeted by knotted strings.

I was bullied by a friend
For five months, until
My best friend put it to an end.
She had the confidence that I was missing
And saved me from someone I thought would look out for me.
We all go through things as a part of living.

But you need to know - there is someone there for you
A parent, friend, teacher or one of the many others,
Someone there to help you start anew.
You just need to look
Through the murky mist
For help can be found, even if in a book

Hannah Coleman (12)
Bishop Ramsey CE School, London Borough Of Hillingdon

Escape

Stop shouting at the TV, they say,
You're having too much screen time, they say,
Use your knife and fork, they say,
Don't kick your ball inside the house, they say.

The world is full of war and conflict, I say,
It is murky, like unclean and polluted water, I say,
There are people with no medical help when they need it, I say,
So let me escape for just a little bit, I say.

Your game contains too much violence, they say,
You have not spent long enough on your homework, they say,
Kids today have it far too easy, they say,
You should appreciate what you have, they say.

Innocent people are dying for no reason, I say,
Towns and cities are turning into war-torn battlefields, I say,
Hurricanes rip homes apart like there's no tomorrow, I say,
So let me escape for just a little bit, I say.

Freddy Lovelock (11)
Bishop Ramsey CE School, London Borough Of Hillingdon

Windrush

As I looked up at the boat,
I felt a lump in my throat,
We were at the port of Tilbury, 1948,
And, just by looking, I could sense many stares of hate,
Once we arrived, I stepped off the ship,
In fear, I bit my lip
So hard that I could taste the tang of blood,
With torn-up shoes, I stepped into the mud,
I thought that this home would actually be nice,
But, according to my eyes, this would have to suffice,
I walked to my slum house,
I couldn't force a single word out of my mouth,
It became a daily chore to listen to racist comments,
It would be weird to not get a few of them a day,
Finally, it was revealed that we were being treated like this,
It was the best days of our lives in 2018,
The day that they introduced the compensation scheme,
Even though we were originally thought of as sick and feeble,
The government had now granted documentation to over 17,000 people!

Matilda Denham-Cuerel (11)
Bishop Ramsey CE School, London Borough Of Hillingdon

Love

Love.
It is a thing that turns the purest bitter
Or the hateful happy.
But the thing love has in common is
It's fragile and could break any second.
If you love for too long,
It could be the cause of all your sadness.
A moment less,
And you could be the pain someone else is suffering.
Lines fade,
Friends, benefits, relationships, heartbreak
It's a repeated cycle
That can make or break your day.
Love is attached to everything.
Hard and delicate at the same time
And makes you see life for life.

Some use love as a game,
When it comes down to it, they can't explain.
Love is trouble but will eventually come,
So just be careful to whom you say you 'love'.
As at the end of the day,
They may not be the one.

Neve Callan-Mordy (13)
Bishop Ramsey CE School, London Borough Of Hillingdon

The Beautiful Truth

We are the same!
There is no difference between me and you
We are all the same
My skin is black and yours is white
But the difference is only the word that you write

I came to this world with blessings from God
I grow with my beliefs, my passion in my heart
And I knew changes would happen in the history card
Yes, this time begins!

The freedom is ours!
I feel this in my veins
My soul wants to start new reigns

I feel like a Pegasus flying towards the sun
Which kisses my face and makes me feel fun
My wings are full of power and hope
And I've stopped feeling my wrist from the horrible rope

Proud of my Black History
So glad that people said sorry
The future is yours
The freedom is ours!

Nicola Wisniewska (11)
Bishop Ramsey CE School, London Borough Of Hillingdon

The Life Of Our Planets And Ourselves

The beautiful truth can be found in the most unlikely of places.
Depending on where we are and all the different faces.
To see the truth is to see what's right for the world and each other,
To see what we must do to stop the thunder.
To see stars underneath us,
There are problems that we need to discuss.
To learn, to grow and to understand what needs to be done,
We need to know that this Earth is the only one.
As we started as a star and will end as a symbol of bright light,
For that, in-between, we need to be knights.
Life is the reason we are here and living the dream,
So, to keep it together, we must work as a team.
The beautiful truth can be found in the most unlikely of places,
So, we need to preserve what is left, for the last of the ages.

Sofia McQuaid (11)
Bishop Ramsey CE School, London Borough Of Hillingdon

Are You A Bot?

When playing a game, it is always a blast,
Until the fun becomes a thing of the past.
When you see the dreaded question, you are tied in a knot,
Asking if you're real or if you're a bot.
When you are trying desperately to log into an app,
And you have no time and want it ASAP,
The dreaded question stops you dead on the spot,
'Are you real or are you a bot?'
Whether you are in a meeting or doing work,
You know the question is going to drive you berserk.
From the first comma to the last full stop,
It will ask you, 'Are you real or are you a bot?'
So, in this world of technology and computer stuff,
Logging into things can be quite tough.
I do not care about counting a lamp post, bike or even a tree,
I just want to be authentically me.

Hattie Kimber (11)
Bishop Ramsey CE School, London Borough Of Hillingdon

Is This Me?

Bees are happy,
I am sad,
Birds are peaceful,
I am mad.

Dolphins are smart,
I am not.
I'm nothing like that graceful lot.

Elephants are loud,
I can't shout.
Monkeys can smile,
I just about sulkily pout.

Zebras are stripy,
I'm just plain,
I don't have a majestic lion's mane.

Ants are tiny,
I am tall,
But like a jerboa,
My brain is small.

This was then,
A tortoise hiding away,
Like a dog I was lost,
I'd just gone astray.

As proud as an eagle,
I have the strength to be,
I've found my way,
I'm okay being me.

Aidan O'Connor (11)
Bishop Ramsey CE School, London Borough Of Hillingdon

Whispers Of A Crying Earth

Earth, once lush, being battered on repeat,
Climate change's toll is a challenge to meet,
Seas rise high and oceans roar,
Nature's plea, we can no longer ignore.

Fierce storms rage, with untamed might,
Eroding landscapes, day and night,
Forests burn, and species disappear,
The time to act is drawing near.

Let's heed the call, every woman and man,
Reduce emissions wherever we can,
Renewable energy, a path to explore,
A sustainable future for generations more.

Together, let's stand, for only one planet we have,
Take action now for life to thrive,
For Earth's sake, let's make it right,
Ensure a future for generations is bright.

David Dudday (14)
Bishop Ramsey CE School, London Borough Of Hillingdon

From Porcelain To Power

Anger surged through her,
Turning the cockles in her mind,
Tired, button eyes rewind,
Unravelling threads,
Of a carefully spun tale,
To retell the unheard.

Cracking her picture-perfect mask,
Disguise is unveiled,
All hail the break of silence.

For every lost dream we scream,
Ruin their peace,
Pieces of porcelain scatter the floor,
"To be seen and not heard,"
We rise from the shards,
Defiant, loud, bold,
Revolution has occurred.

She cut the strings of her marionette heart,
Dancing free in a world,
Where she writes her own part.

Melat Mengsh (16)
Bishop Ramsey CE School, London Borough Of Hillingdon

To Be A Girl

How have the standards of a generation
Changed by the impact of social media?
Women half-clothed, plastered everywhere you look,
A flat stomach and 'perfect body' seem to be the beauty standard.
How could this degeneracy be so accepted by our society?
The change from those 60 years ago,
Who knew that the choice of a partner was not because of their body,
But was unconditional.
So why can we not have this now?
The human body is meant to have body hair and fat to protect us,
But this is considered disgusting.
Society needs to look at itself and change.

Kyle Didd (16)
Bishop Ramsey CE School, London Borough Of Hillingdon

The World We Live In

We live in a world with
things going on like bullying, racism and countries
at war

So many different people, some rich, some poor
Underneath our skin, we are all just the same
So why do we live in a world full of blame?

Why can't people just get along?
No name-calling, no bullying
Just have some fun

We are in a world with so many people
We should all stick together through
thick and thin
And all come together to dance and sing

It makes me sad 'cause it gets worse
each day
So, let's all come together to sit and pray.

Harley Ellis (11)
Bishop Ramsey CE School, London Borough Of Hillingdon

Separation

Remember the day you were turned down,
The time your face showed only a frown,
The wind brushed through your hair,
Trapping you inside this lonely lair,
Then a glint of sunshine touched your eye,
And all those worries evaporated into the sky,
Your face was full of laughter and pride,
Your heart was full on either side.

Megan Gulian (12)
Bishop Ramsey CE School, London Borough Of Hillingdon

I Lost Me

All their gazes are on me,
Where I go, eyes follow me,
Start doubting me,
Am I too awkward in a large crowd?
Or too annoying and loud?
I look down,
Maybe I can see myself in the mirror in front of me,
I can't see me,
Look to my left, the car window hides all of me,
Am I invisible or fake?
I long to become one of them,
Part of them,
So they can't stare at me,
Laugh with them,
Hang out with them,
But I lost me,
This is not me.

Faked me.

Halaa Takafi
City College, Norwich

To The Shadows

In the shadows where our secrets stay,
The overwhelming feeling of guilt comes into play,
Truths we dare not to speak,
Collide with our barriers begging for peace.

The aching feeling inside overpowers,
Taking over the life that was once ours,
Not being able to contain the lies,
Every truth from every lie starts to rise.

The words spill out into the open,
No secret left unspoken,
No lie left concealed,
As a wave of words leaves everything revealed.

There used to be secrets staying in our shadows' depths,
Now there's light shining through since finding peace within ourselves.
The guilt used to dominate,
But now we've been set free of that unwanted weight.

In the shadows where guilt and lies once stood,
Stand truth and happiness.

Erin Griffiths (13)
Cornelius Vermuyden, Canvey Island

The Ugly Truth

Behind her mask, there is peace at last,
But a lie is blocking her past,
Memories lost, the truth be told,
As there's a guilt she has to hold,
A grey cloud hung at her head,
She has to put this guilt to bed,
Her palms are sweating,
It's blocking her head,
She feels uneasy thumping in her ears,
Her heart is full of fear,
The time is up, she has to hear,
But she might start to tear,
She goes to say, but she's blocked,
With a pit in her stomach,
She feels ill,
Almost like she had killed,
With a heavy heart,
They were torn apart,
They lost their spark,
And it wasn't long until it all went dark,
No thoughts,
No feelings,
This one lie felt like she had died,
But she didn't, she fainted, her life was fake-ish.

Sophie Roddy (12)
Cornelius Vermuyden, Canvey Island

When I Was A Little Kid

At six we were small
Went on our tiptoes to stand tall
We acted like mothers
And loved wearing vibrant colours

At ten we grew up
No longer drank out of a baby cup
We loved playing sport
And we were no longer short

At thirteen we switched
Our voices weren't as high-pitched
We didn’t like school
And things we loved before were uncool

At sixteen we missed when we were young
Before posing, we stuck out our tongues
Wondering what we would become
Wanting to be a mum

As a kid, my parents told me their childhood story
And all their history
Now I tell my kids what I did
When I was a little kid.

Baylee Pamphilon (12)
Cornelius Vermuyden, Canvey Island

What Is Truth?

What is truth? Is it black or white?
Or is it all colours to be seen, day or night?
When you look at someone, what do you see?
A lie or the truth - which could it be?
When you wake up in the morning is this reality,
And the people around you, are they really trustworthy?
When you look for the answer, is it false or is it true,
And is it just our eyes but is the sky really blue?
Why do we want the truth to be told?
Who knows when we're hot we could actually be cold.
When you think of the truth, what do you see?
And when you look in the mirror is it you, or is it me?

Sienna Ross (11)
Cornelius Vermuyden, Canvey Island

Journey Through The Flaws

In the weave of journeys we take,
Every stumble brings us closer to wake.
With every fall, we learn to rise,
Finding strength in these imperfect skies.

Through the roads of worry, flaws and fear,
We focus on the hope and peace that is near.
We embrace the mistakes, the cracks of our lives
And find the beauty that life offers, even when we must strive.

Behind the traffic, behind the noise,
We must find our truth, find our voice.
Behind our defective, imperfect journeys,
We will find our beautiful destination.

Hollie Gerrish (12)
Cornelius Vermuyden, Canvey Island

Nature All Around

Nature all around, shining with the trees
Nature all around, crying all her words
Nature all around, she lies on gracious grounds
Mother Nature mocks us with her beauty
Like a radiant golden statue
She stares lovingly, her arms open wide
But what really matters is what is inside
Her hopes are that the world won't fail
She believes in people
Her love everlasting
She loves us all, so crowns us with her glory
This is love
A love that will never die.

Charley Hardy (11)
Cornelius Vermuyden, Canvey Island

The Hallway

The lights are flickering,
The walls are chipped.
I've never seen anything like this.
The floor is broken,
I really hope this will be my token.
I want to see what's in that door wide open.

She went in, it was like looking in a mirror,
All the colours, all the sounds.
She was happy now, she had finally found herself.

Ruby Savage (12)
Cornelius Vermuyden, Canvey Island

Ready, Steady, Jump

Tack up the horse
Getting ready to ride
My feelings of excitement, I just can't hide
He starts to warm up
With his majestic walk
Moving on to a trot
My belly in knots
Clip-clopping along
I don't want to get this wrong
Ready... steady... *jump!*

Lily May (11)
Cornelius Vermuyden, Canvey Island

Beautiful Emotions

Beautiful emotions are happy,
Beautiful emotions are sad,
Beautiful emotions are fearful,
Beautiful emotions are anger,
Beautiful emotions make nice people.
Sometimes they can be bad too.
Never be mad at beautiful emotions.

Amelia-Rose Pulfer (11)
Cornelius Vermuyden, Canvey Island

Truth

T rustworthy, my friends are to me,
R espected is how I want others to feel,
U nderstanding is my family,
T houghtful to others,
H onest is what I am.

Amelia Wood (13)
Cornelius Vermuyden, Canvey Island

What A Beautiful World!

Roses might be red
Violets might be blue
But inside no one can change you!

People in the world come in all shapes and sizes
But I still found you.

Madison Haste (11)
Cornelius Vermuyden, Canvey Island

Whispers

A long train ride to my doom and end
Why do such nice people have to attend
I couldn't think of anything worse
But I hope at least there are fireworks

As the place I once knew
Grew further and further away
To my mother, there were words
That I wanted to say

I woke up in a miserable place
Of hunger and misplace
Appeared on my arm, a tattoo... red,
Cut and swollen, from where it bled.

A stranger led me into this chamber
Encircled by this deadly vapour
Just longing for my final whispers
To be heard by somebody new.

Tamyia Skelsey (12)
Dane Court Grammar School, Broadstairs

The Truth About Others

You don't know how he feels,
You don't know what he's done,
You don't know what he cares about,
Winter or burning sun,
You don't know what's in his mind,
Or what he loves the most,
But search deeper still and all you'll find is that it's all a hoax,
You know how he feels,
You know what he's done,
You know what's in his mind,
And you don't like what you find,
Who knew this innocent little boy could be such a criminal mastermind?

Joel Bongers (11)
Glyn School, Ewell

Monster

"Oh my gosh, look at her!" the children exclaim,
"She looks like a monster!"
"Ewww."
"Monster..."
Monster?
The 'monster' cried after that,
Tears streaming down her face,
The words replaying in her mind, "She looks like a monster!"
It happened the next day,
And the next,
And the next,
And then she never left her room,
"Oh, the monster's back in her cave," the children laughed,
And then she stopped showing up at school,
"Where is she?" muttered the children,
"Have you ever thought how you made her feel?" the teacher spoke,
"Have you ever even wanted to worry about her?" the teacher said,
"Maybe that's why she never leaves her 'cave',"
Because that's where she feels normal,
Because that's where she feels safe,
Because that's where she can be herself,
Not worrying about the names,

Think before you speak,
You don't know what someone is going through.

Suzie Milton-Harris (12)
Kingsbury School, Kingsbury

Thoughts

She perches next to her heap of guilt, aged 35, about to crack
How did it leave me, and why did it happen?
It faded away
I didn't mean it
I didn't mean to
She screams
She smashes her forehead against her empty wall, soaked with guilty blood
Drip, drip, drip, it leaks down the pale of the paint
She taps her finger against her lip; she looks down at it and sighs
She touches her chest, her ribs thin with hate, worn down to the bone
She grinds herself away until there are no more
Her cartoon heart beating visible to the eye, her cheeks stained with tears
Oh God, oh God, help me
She clasps her hands together and pleads
I will do anything, please, oh please
Silence
Her knees buckle and break beneath her as she falls to the floor
I'm sorry
A tear ambles down her scared and beaten face
Gulp
It's too much. What did I do to deserve this?

Her voice coarse and broken
It went too far, the darkness, the hate
I tried to stop them
She searches around her gloomy pit, nowhere to go, nowhere to hide
She's surrounded by people who care, but in a way she's alone
Wrapped up in her past
She throws herself against the empty floor, letting her head bounce
The ringing in her ears relentless, she let her arms spread out wide
All the thoughts compress into a tiny ball, so tight they can't contain any more
The elastic band is about to snap
And she struggles to fight back
Drowning in her tears, smothered in self-hate
You see, she liked to be alone
Sitting on the sidelines
Watching every thought and feeling pass her by
Some days they'd poke and make fun
She's not good enough
She'll always be alone
But in her mind, it was just a game
No need to feed into their lies
Score; 1-0
But that wouldn't do; they need more points
And they'd joke and laugh, pointing fingers

But they still couldn't win
So it became a competition; they'd kick her down for days at a time
Beat her till her mind went numb
Last man standing
Survival of the fittest
They'd run laps and laps around her brain
She simply couldn't keep up
Until one day everything went quiet
All her thoughts, all her feelings melted away
There was no more room left to care
So now she sits on her kitchen floor, wishing she didn't let them win
Wishing she had let someone help her
Because maybe she didn't have to fight her battles all on her own.

Jamie-Rose Sellar (13)
Kingsbury School, Kingsbury

Geek: A Definition

If you were to ask me why I'm unique
You could say my disability, but if I were to speak
I would say that I'm a geek

What I mean is, for example, although I like to cook
You'll mostly see me with my nose in a comic book
I know almost every character and their names
Everything they've been in, from movies to games

About video games, I also know much,
Playing Minecraft, Arkham City, and such
Roaming wastelands, plains, asylums too
When I'm glued to the bed, and can't bother to move

I must say, as well, it is my duty
For every so often to watch great movies
That might be where my love for movie-making comes from
I'll watch any genre, but please not rom-com

If there are iconic characters, and someone goes, who's that?
I'll be honest, it kind of makes me mad
But I do get some characters are really obscure
Who are they, apart from me, no one's really sure

So, what have we learned, what's a geek, what could it be?
I'll tell you in one word: me.

Archie Richards (14)
Kingsbury School, Kingsbury

Recovery

A prisoner of my own mind,
Clad in rusted, anguished armour,
Ridiculed by my own thoughts,
The weight of the world buried me alive,
Everything seemed like a hurdle that could not be overcome,
Locked in my own skin...

Until you gave me the key,
Defended me against my thoughts,
Made my obscene life a normal one,
Lifted the sky from my weary shoulders,
You became everything I'd ever wished for,
But that's what you wanted me to think...

Then you left a knife in my back,
Tore me open, exposed to the cold,
Crushed me with the weight of the world,
Abandoned and alone,
Left in anguish,
I bled in silence,
The memory of your maim voice,
Still brings me to malaise.

Denial...
I stood there, dumbfounded,
Surely you'd never do that to me,
You loved me,
Didn't you?
I still love you,
It's not fair,
It's never been fair.

Anger...
I hate you like fire hates rain,
I want you to feel the same agony I suffered in,
I am torn like paper and long to shred you,
I'm boiling with rage and want to burn you,
I'm a storm brewing on the horizon,
I will destroy you.

Bargaining...
I miss you,
I-I'm sorry,
Please... take me back,
It's all my fault,
I regret every word, every tear,
I suppose I overreacted,
Surely you weren't that bad,
Surely it's all in my head,
Isn't it?

Depression...
I'll never find love,
I never should have let you go,
I feel like a ghost,
Condemned to haunt my lonely room,
My aptitude of overthinking is not helpful,
Happiness appears to be a mere hoax,
I'll never be able to carry on without you,
Will I?

Acceptance...
Fooled by your beguiling act,
Led to believe I was nothing without you,
But now I know,
I know you never deserved me,
I have the scars to prove it,
I have the support to know I'm worth more,
My wounds are now silver scars,
Healed and reminders of my strength,
I am whole again,
I've been pieced back together,
And will never let anyone tear me apart again.

Libby-May Mullaley (13)
Kingsbury School, Kingsbury

Truth Behind Someone

Gasping for air among the distorted voices
Negative thoughts fill my brain within seconds
Zoning out because I'm too scared to cry
"Are you okay? You've not been like yourself for weeks," they ask

I hate that question
I cry instead of trying to open up
I ignore them because I don't want help
But I want better mental health
I want to tell people I'm okay

With tears in my eyes, I say, "I'm okay"
Instead, I tell my favourite teacher my emotions
They actually help me
I don't want my best friend or parents worrying about me

They say, "Time will heal itself"
But I've waited 5 years to heal
Maybe this is what I deserve
I feel isolated, and not cared about by anyone

Maybe I won't be happy in school
Maybe I'll stay stressed, alone, sad
Maybe I deserve to live like this
Or maybe I'll live to see me in my dream job with the happiness of a family.

Lexi Cartwright (12)
Kingsbury School, Kingsbury

The Beautiful Game

I was five when I first touched the ball,
Kicking it against the wall, just down the hall.
Bare feet on concrete, I'd dream, I'd play,
That one day I'd wear the colours, run away.

On rainy fields, where grass kissed the sky,
I learned to fall, to leap, to fly.
With every bruise, I felt the pain,
But in every fall, I rose again.

The neighbourhood games, with no lines drawn,
Where the goals were jackets, and we'd play till dawn.
No crowd, no cheers, just us and the street,
But in my mind, it was Wembley at my feet.

I practised until my legs felt sore,
Dribbling past shadows, always wanting more.
The taste of victory, the sting of loss,
Each lesson learned came at a cost.

Then came the scouts, eyes wide as they stared,
I felt the weight, but I wasn't scared.
A chance, a call, to play for the team,
The jersey fit like a forgotten dream.

The training was tough, the drills were long,
But deep in my heart, the fire was strong.
I'd chase the ball till my lungs would burn,
For the roar of the crowd, I'd always yearn.

The whistle blew, my first real game,
I stepped on the pitch, nothing felt the same.
The noise, the lights, the sea of faces,
I ran like the wind, I found my places.

The years flew by, seasons came and went,
Every goal, every pass, each moment spent.
Through wins and losses, I learned my way,
And I still wake up for the love of play.

Now, I stand here, on this field of green,
A boy with a dream, who lived the scene.
From backyard games to the world's great stage,
Football is more than a game – it's my page.

Riley Atherton-Smith (12)
Kingsbury School, Kingsbury

Our 2023 Life

Twelve months deep into 2023, Here are all the memes from.
January, Queen Bee singing in Dubai filmed illegally, Selena vs Hailey Cat in Schiaparelli.
February, Harry got the Grammy, Sly Balloon Rihanna hit Choreo with a human in her womb, Ariana DeBose spit bars lit the room, Ice Spice hit hard duh, duh, duh, made a boom.
March, Toast Man Eras Tour began everybody freaking out about a TikTok ban.
April, AI got out of control, Barbie posters were posted by every local.
May, the Renaissance Tour by Bey Met Gala was a problematic slay, British man gets a hat at his little party, Kim K in an AHS play.
June, Alexa Play No Air by Jordan Sparks, billionaires got lost down with the sharks, Miranda's ukulele got completely torn apart, Twitter lives its last month, Grimace had us by the heart.
July, NPCs were a big deal that back there isn't real, Cardi threw the microphone Nair guy made us squeal, UFO, Ariana and SpongeBob steal.
August, Kanye on about showing us boat brawl, Lisso called out, but she hits back, lots of Nicki flooding Call of Duty maps, Trump mugshots hit Joe double taps.
September, the Roman Empire hit the street, men throwing balls at the Taylor meet and greet.
October, Peta had some arcade fun, bedbugs had Remy's favourite city overrun.

November, remember Harry now he's hairless, remember TikTok now it's all just this, Zac and Cody finally made it off the waiting list, Nate Jacobs's bathwater, Jenna is a true sis. December, Pink Friday's pink town, Santos got the kick, diva down diva done, the Senate Hearing room is now only hearing clapping sounds, Gypse made a kicking exit from the prison grounds.

Jack Ault (14)
Kingsbury School, Kingsbury

A Girl's Journey Of Becoming A Chef

In the future, when schooldays end,
A single dream I'll still defend:
To be a chef, to cook and create,
New recipes on every plate.

Together in the kitchen's glow,
Crafting dishes, watch them grow.
Cooking for others, vibrant and bright,
Each meal a canvas, a colourful sight.

Meeting people, sharing cheer,
In every dish, my dream is clear.
To cook, to serve, to make anew,
This is the dream I'll pursue.

In a kitchen filled with scents so sweet,
Where flavours dance and spices meet,
A dream is born, a passion grows,
In the heart of one who truly knows.

With every chop and every stir,
A symphony of tastes occur,
From humble roots to gourmet heights,
A chef's journey ignites the nights.

The sizzle of the pan, the boil of the pot,
In every dish, a story's plot,
From farm to table, sea to shore,
A chef's love for food is evermore.

In the heat of the kitchen, dreams take flight,
Crafting meals from morning till night,
With passion, skill and endless zest,
A chef's journey is truly blessed.

Through trials and errors, flavours blend,
Towards culinary dreams that never end.
Each ingredient tells its own tale,
In this culinary voyage we sail.

For in each bite, there lies a chance,
To make the heart and soul dance.
So here's to dreams of plates and pans,
Of soups and sauces, pots and flans.
For in the kitchen's steady hum,
The chef's true calling has just begun.

Rosalyn Clarke (11)
Kingsbury School, Kingsbury

Turning Inside Out

Inspired by the movie Inside Out

Sometimes I wonder, what if I was Riley?
What if I had these people in my head?
What if my head was the one they'd chosen?

Would Joy be at the control panel
Or would it be Sadness, or maybe Fear?
Possibly Anger or even Disgust
But would they be locked in that jar?
What if a new emotion took over
One I had never felt before?

Would Joy's yellow glow flicker and dim
Or would it shine brighter than ever?
Would Disgust grow sharper and turn up her nose
Not only at broccoli but at the dark side of society?
And then there'd be Anger, burning hot and getting redder
His flames bursting out of his head
Or would he be cool and calm
And not get angry at anything?

Would Sadness be at the controls
Her fingers sinking into every memory?
She wouldn't be there, though
That's not a possibility
Unless I've had a bad day
She's just there; not really the main character
And lastly, the quiet one: Fear

He wouldn't come out much
He'd always be there when he's needed
Always out of the way when he's not.

Inside Out turns my thoughts inside out
My head might be full of these emotions
But, in the end, Joy is always the one in control
Always the one to keep me
In a good mood.

Isla Cook (12)
Kingsbury School, Kingsbury

Trapped

Day and night I lie awake, motivation lost
Ceiling is pretty, my thoughts run wild
Though I think with my desolate mind
My feet dragging me out of my bed

I sit, in my desolate room
No light, no music. Killed everyone? Wake up.
Throw clothes on, shouting overwhelming
I feel it all but nothing too

At hell I arrive and wait, I wait
One step, shirt. Another step, coat
Blazer on, coat off, shirt tucked, jumper off.
I feel it all but nothing too

They are evil minds that cause destruction
Sorcerer of Death's construction
Trapped and puppets of mankind
Poisoning their brainwashed minds

Want it or not but need it, yes
Poison and strain on the brain
Clouding in like a nightmare with no escape
All felt but yet nothing felt too

Finally, it's over, I walk away
Messages sent, letters mailed in dawn opened in dusk
Homework left due, yet no sanction to be given
Felt all yet nothing too

At hell, I arrive and wait
Evil minds that cause destruction
Sorcerers of Death's construction
Back into my desolate mind

Into sleep, I fall deep
Drowning in my overwhelming thoughts
I feel empty yet so full
Pricked with a knife or other

I feel everything, yet I feel nothing at all
(I'm a-okay).

Alisha Dolman (15)
Kingsbury School, Kingsbury

Moment Of Bliss

This is a thing of perfection,
It's part of me when I look at my reflection,
Cookies and cream,
The definition of my dream.

When the wrapper opens up,
I brighten like a buttercup,
The blue packaging that can't escape my eagle eye,
The blue packaging that lifts my spirits sky high.

I dash over like The Flash,
(Careful not to crash),
I've now stolen the pack,
And you've lost your snack.

The fridge is my next pit stop,
Though I have to reach right for the top,
I persist as the white liquid cannot be forgotten,
I just cross my fingers and hope it's not rotten.

Alas, I have obtained the white fluid,
My hopes shall not be ruined.
To the top I fill the glass,
For I am a girl of class.

Finally, sprawled out across the bed,
Content knowing I'm about to be fed,
I dunk the round bliss in,
(Seriously, what a win).

Cautious, so it doesn't sink like an anchor,
As cautious as a banker,
However, to my delight,
I have been spared the fright.

Greedily, I gobble it whole
For I am a hungry, hungry mole,
As expected, the taste is lovely like silk,
That is why I love Oreos and milk.

Lia Jones (15)
Kingsbury School, Kingsbury

Stereotypes

Stereotypes linger like shadows,
Boxes were placed in,
Labels stuck,
Defining us by the surface.

The suit and tie,
A marker of success,
But inside,
A heart beats a different rhythm.

The athlete,
Powerful yet tender,
Misunderstood,
Dreams hidden beneath the roar of applause.

The introvert,
Quiet in a crowded room,
A world unfolding,
In the silence rich and vast,
But often overlooked.

The artist,
Paint splattered and wild,
Labelled as impractical,
Yet crafting truths,
That cut deeper than any score.

We forget the stories,
The layers beneath the surface,
The laughter, the pain,
The hopes that soar.

To see each other's world,
Not through a layer of assumption,
But with open hearts,
Inviting everyone,
Into the conversation.

Let us step beyond the shadows,
Embrace the beautiful chaos,
And celebrate the diverse tapestry,
Woven from countless threads,
Each one essential,
Each one unique.

Willow Passey (12)
Kingsbury School, Kingsbury

Never Give Up!

If you get pushed down,
Try and get back up,
Don't think you have to stop,
When you could push a little harder,
And get to the top.

When something is hard and you're finding it difficult,
Don't look down, don't give up,
Keep going, you can do it,
Don't think you're stuck.

Just think,
How amazing it would be to look back one day and think
Wow!
Did I really do that?

You can do it,
So, get back up and try again,
This is your moment.
It's worth the pain.

Be true to yourself,
Never give up!

Anna Spencer (11)
Kingsbury School, Kingsbury

Changes

You have now come to that age,
When things have started to change,

Your favourite colour is no longer pink,
Because it's babyish, and you worry what your friends will think,

You now hate to wear your rainbow shoes,
Because what will your friends say if they know your mom still has to choose?

You can't wear the best sparkly bow in your hair,
Because you know that your friends won't be able to bear.

You ignore your friend's texts asking you to come,
Because you think you'll just ruin their fun.

The next day they arrive at your door,
With a sparkly bow in one's hair and nothing more,
The other has on a pair of rainbow shoes, a pair that their mum had to choose,
And the last in complete pink,
Not the slightest care about what the others would think,

The world suddenly seems to brighten,
As all the darkness vanishes behind you,
And the path ahead enlightens.

Ariella Hodgkins (11)
Kingsbury School, Kingsbury

Genesis

I tremble as I walk with severed vines trailing behind me
I shiver but I'm not cold
I'm full but I feel so empty

I carry on though each step I take the vines resist and pull me back
I walk on a straight cobbled path
I'm surrounded but I feel so alone

I realise the vines are snakes that are tightening themselves around me
I feel them pass through me like a phantom
I'm real but I feel so fake

I see an end to this long pathway
I push with all my strength but I still fail
I'm trying so hard but failing so miserably

I find a mausoleum with a weeping angel statue leaning against my grave
I know who's inside
I'm dead but I'm alive

I feel the tension on my body loosen as the snakes slither away turning into stone carvings on the grave
I sit next to myself then suddenly the statue crumbles and the angel is reborn
I'm gone but there is a new genesis.

AJ Clarke (13)
Kingsbury School, Kingsbury

Great...

"Great, more friends! More social life!"
It's always great at first, then it slows...
"They're not answering my texts. They must be busy!"
Maybe busy, maybe not. But you get this weird feeling of intuition that something's wrong.
"Oh, they've posted. Oh, they're with them... that's fine! They have other friends!"
Social media helps, but doesn't. It shows their pros, but also their cons.
"Let's see... okay, at this point, I don't care what they do."
Then you drift away and it's for the best, they weren't the best and you weren't a match.
Now you don't remember, and it's been a couple of years, you heard they haven't changed.
Now trust me, you're happy you left them be.
Just leave them there, in their lair, and leave happy as can be.

Elsie Kelly (11)
Kingsbury School, Kingsbury

The Beauty Of Space

Space is fascinating,
Space is beautiful,
People find it boring,
But I find it cool.

Space amazes me truly,
It may bore other people,
They just don't see what I see,
They just need to see the sky twinkle.

Way up in the galaxies,
Way up high,
With the loss of gravity,
Watching shooting stars fly by.

Blast off goes the rocket,
On its journey to the moon,
Dodging all of the comets,
Arriving at their destination soon.

Daydreaming into space,
Thinking of all its wonders,
While I'm up in the Milky Way,
Watching everybody that's under.

Stargazing with my telescope,
Pointing at all the constellations,
Wondering how the stars float,
Using my imagination,
That's just the beauty of space.

Olivia Henderson (13)
Kingsbury School, Kingsbury

Unveiling The Heart

In shadows cast by doubt and fear
The beautiful truth begins to clear
A gentle light that softly glows
Revealing paths where honesty flows

It whispers softly in the light
Guiding hearts towards the light
With every word, a bond is made
In vulnerability, we aren't afraid

Like petals opening to the sun
In shared moments, we become one
Authenticity, a precious thread
Weaving stories that need to be said

In laughter shared and tears that fall
The beautiful truth unites us all
A tapestry rich with colours bright
In the fabric of life, we find our light

So let us speak, let us be bold
In every truth, a story unfolds
For in the journey of hearts laid bare
We find the beauty that's truly rare.

Heidi-Mai Guest (14)
Kingsbury School, Kingsbury

Friendly Football Fun

No one likes to not have fun
it's like shoelaces, if they're not done up it can't be fun to walk with you tripping up over again.
The key is no matter what happens to you the other players playing do not need you releasing your anger on them
if you don't win the ball.
Also, if you get injured, it does not mean you need to hurt them back.
Would you like to be injured?
No.
It may be an accident but you can get back by getting up
and scoring or doing a good skill on them to get a laugh
and after the match you can have a quick chat with them.
If they do it on purpose it does not matter because if the ref sees it they will discipline them for their actions
no matter what you do not injure anyone to stay on the good side.

Toby Gilfeather (11)
Kingsbury School, Kingsbury

Nature's Welcome

In the still of the night, the full moon gleams,
Its silver light dancing on the tranquil streams.
Reflections shimmer on the water's face,
A serene moment a peaceful embrace.

The sky above, a canvas of deep blue,
Starry companions scattered like dew.
The sky stretches wide, a vast open view,
Where dreams take flight and hopes are anew.

Beyond the water's surface, deep down below,
Roots begin to form, a tree starts to grow.
Peeking out, reaching to the sky,
The leaves shimmer on a turquoise high.

Under the stars where dreams intertwine,
We dance under moonlight and everything aligns.
Tranquillity flows when in nature's welcome,
To experience it once is to experience heaven.

Grace Thompson-Moore (14)
Kingsbury School, Kingsbury

Welcome To Sport!

Welcome to the world of sport,
There's many things to like,
Football, tennis, hockey, swimming,
And even riding your bike!

Zoom! there goes Usain Bolt,
He's running incredibly fast,
Nobody can catch up to him,
You can't seem to get past.

Welcome to the world of sport,
There's always something entertaining,
Rugby, cricket, baseball, boxing,
Joe Root that's gonna sting!

Muhammad Ali is in the ring,
I think he might've won,
Ronaldinho is on the wing,
With his tricks, he is not quite done.

Welcome to the world of sport,
There's many things to like,
Basketball, sailing, diving, racing,
And even doing a hike!

Luca Salisbury (12)
Kingsbury School, Kingsbury

What's Going On With You?

M y name is Georgia Ferris and this is my story!
Y ou don't know the real me; I don't know how to make the right friends, taking it too seriously.

P robably going to end up in the bumps.
"R ight, I'm fed up with you."
O rigins feel like they're failing one day at a time, thanks to anxiety.
B egging for forgiveness, having no other person to go to.
"L oser, loser two times in a row." I can't just let it go.
E veryone looking at you. "I *need* to go, get me out!"
M e, it's always me, I'm the problem, why oh why is it me?
"S top!" I can't, it's who I am and I can't stop.

Believe in who you are!

Georgia Ferris (11)
Kingsbury School, Kingsbury

Music Is Everything

Music is the air in my lungs
On days I feel like I'm suffocating.
Melodies are like lifejackets
To stop me from sinking when I'm unable to swim.
Beats are like my heart, pounding in my ears.
Music makes me who I am.

Strings look like the veins running through my body,
Percussion is the sound of my feet as I walk.
Woodwind is my heavy sighs after a long day.
Music makes me who I am.

Waterfalls, like the flowing melody of a piano piece.
Ragged earth, like rock songs.
Leaves rustle, like old guitar strings
Yet they crunch like clean new ones.

Music is nature,
Music is life.
Music makes up everything.
Music makes me, me.

Maggie Milton-Harris (14)
Kingsbury School, Kingsbury

The Giraffe In A Pickle!

One day, a giraffe went to a magical witch.
"Oh hey, Miss Witch, I'm in a pickle!"
"Oh, no worries, what is the problem?"
The giraffe stared at her in disbelief.
"I just told you, I'm in a pickle!"
The witch, who looked puzzled, said,
"Well, okay, but please be aware of Vector The Despicable!"
The giraffe questioned her on who Vector was,
but then she stated she was told rumours
and she had to spread them or she would get tickled.

After a few hours of chatting,
a few hours of yapping,
The witch went outside and saw a giraffe inside a pickle!
"Uh-oh, I'm so sorry!"

Abigail Birch (12)
Kingsbury School, Kingsbury

Keep Going

When the road is long and skies are grey,
And the sun seems far, so far away.
Remember, storms will always pass,
And new days break from shattered glass.

Each step you take, though slow and small,
Will lead you where you're meant to fall.
For mountains tall are meant to climb,
And courage grows with every climb.

So rise again, though tired and worn,
For in your soul, new strength is born.
The path ahead, though rough, may be,
Will lead you to your victory.

Keep going, friend, don't lose your fight,
For even in the darkest night,
There's always hope, there's always light,
And in your heart, you'll find what's right.

Dorian Popescu (12)
Kingsbury School, Kingsbury

Autumnal Breeze

Hues of deep cardinal, the darling reds
Envelop tree leaves as they softly fall,
Crying to each other as the blush spreads
And lightens the veins, a seasonal call.
Lone choir that the sweet, joyous songbirds sing,
Praise to her paradise, heavenly bliss.
The far-off church dings, the brass bells still rings,
A chime for the sun, as the gold rays kiss
The earth, dappling the dry ground with shadows
And light. A mixture of love and death dim,
Foreseen in the coming winter sorrows
Which make the world grow sad. Autumn holds his
Head up proud, not humble or vain, and makes
Plentiful light shed on Winter's mistakes.

Kacey Cooke (14)
Kingsbury School, Kingsbury

Facing The Bombs

Facing the bombs, I would rather do
Than sit here alone
Stuck with you
Evacuee girl, in a world so unkind
May peace and love
Be the solace I find
Beaten and bruised
Inside and out
I need to come home
Without a doubt
Through the misty window
I long to escape
From the torment and fear
My spirit to reshape
Alone in my sorrow
I dreamed of the day
When freedom would come
And darkness would fade
My courage unbroken
My spirit unbowed
In the face of adversity
I stand proud
So still in pain
I hop on a train
And set off back home
Where I'm no longer alone.

Zoe Salt (13)
Kingsbury School, Kingsbury

Shadows

Wherever you walk,
They follow.
Anywhere and everywhere,
No matter where you are,
They are there.

Chasing your footsteps
Around your city.
Walking with you,
Beside you at every angle,
They creep.

Even when you don't see them,
Or least expect it,
They wander around you
And silently stroll at any time,
They follow.

Copying your every move,
Even at your first sight.
At dawn to dusk,
In the sun or darkness,
They watch.

No one knows what they are doing,
But knows they are busy.
Every person has one question,
What are they?

Ruby Howell (11)
Kingsbury School, Kingsbury

Friends

Friends are like diamonds, they are all adored and wanted.
Diamonds come in every colour of the rainbow,
Friends come in every perfect way.
Diamonds can't melt in lava,
Trust can't melt with a friend.
Both diamonds and friends alike,
Their beauty never ends.

Friends remind me of chocolate,
Both are so lovely and sweet.
A bite of chocolate may be exciting,
So is making a friend.
No matter how long it lasts,
The happiness never ends.
When your friends leave,
Their kindness doesn't,
Like when you finish a chocolate,
Its taste can still be found.

Tilly Farmer (12)
Kingsbury School, Kingsbury

The White Shirt

All my life I wore a green top with blue stripes,
It was cute and all, but it was itchy, annoying,
And made me feel really insecure,
Plus, everyone always laughed at me for it and never accepted me,
One day, when I went to the thrift shop, I saw this beauty of a top,
A white one with so much detail and patterns,
I bought it, and when I wore it, guess what?
I got compliments on it, it was so cool,
Even the girls that used to bully me liked it,
Turns out, I love that top and always will,
Now I have many more clothes,
Pink ones, yellow ones, orange ones,
And so much more.

Lily Hathaway (13)
Kingsbury School, Kingsbury

True To Me

Enjoy spending time with your friends,
Have fun and don't be afraid,
Reminisce on the memories made.

Don't be too hard on yourself,
You're still learning and growing,
Embrace the change, face your fears, take the risks,
Communicate and connect with others.

Talk to people – you are not alone,
Don't worry about the future,
Don't stay stuck in the past,
Live in this world, not your own,

Take deep breaths and focus,
What others think is irrelevant,
Don't doubt everything you do,
Help the people you never knew.

Megan O'Donnell (14)
Kingsbury School, Kingsbury

My Favourite Sport

I saw a poster which led me to my team.
When I joined, my face gleamed.
Now I have joined, I am happy as can be.
Up and down the ball bounces, you see.

Pass, pass, pass, we scored.
Miss, miss, miss, they scored.
Break, we wait.
Who will score the next ball?

Back on the court,
Who will score?
Time will tick.
We best be quick.

Score, score, score,
The crowd roar.
Hip, hip, hooray,
We're on the way.

Now on top,
We got the net.
We are the best.
We won the rest.

Mikey Dolman (11)
Kingsbury School, Kingsbury

My Round-Like-A-Barrel Beagle

I've got a pet beagle
No, not like any other one you know
She likes a bit of treacle
She thinks she's as fast as an eagle
But some people say this fat is illegal
Maybe she was meant to be a seagull?
She's as smelly as a sneezle
Crafty as a weasel
She sure is gleeful
When she takes a bite of meatballs

Although, no one can deny
She's as cheeky as a monkey
As speedy as a snail
But she picks up the pace
And goes on a goose chase
Whenever she spots the fisherman's bait!

Sophie Stinton (13)
Kingsbury School, Kingsbury

Ducks

The ugly duck saw a cook,
The cook was reading a book on how to cook ducks,
The duck started to panic and didn't want to look,
The cook looked at the duck,
And the duck's back started to quiver and his legs shivered,
He fell down a crack,
And the duck said, "Oh quack,"
The cook came out and gave him a smack,
Then the cook took the duck to the book,
To show him how to cook,
Then they became good friends, and wrote lots of books,
About how to cook everything,
Except for ducks!

Harry Geoghan (13)
Kingsbury School, Kingsbury

The Journey To New Adventures

From the oldest to the youngest,
The confidence to worry,
Hopeful hearts and nervous smiles,
We step into our future.

Each turn I take, a brand-new place,
Whispers of laughter fill the air,
And new friendships start to pair.

Yet the worry flies, high as a kite,
With all my steps, I make my way
To this school I'm here to stay.

So here's to change, opening new opportunities,
The guiding light of my future,
I find my place,
Every step I take, I learn and grow.

Freya Wallace (11)
Kingsbury School, Kingsbury

A Fresh Start

It's the start of another school year,
This school is different,
This time you may be full of fear.

New classrooms, different friends,
What's a tutor? Still don't know.
But don't be scared, we'll soon be at the end.

This will all soon be normal,
Calm down, breathe in and out,
Chin up, and act formal.

After all, it's just some more school,
You've been through this before,
Don't be a fool.

You can do this.

Harry Cheneler (12)
Kingsbury School, Kingsbury

Don't Keep Saying Sorry

I know I've done wrong
Yes, I know we all make mistakes
And sometimes all we just need is a break
A break from reality, a break from me
'Cause sometimes that is the only key

I know I've done right
And I know I should be proud
Or maybe I should take my head out of the clouds
I should stop worrying about expectations because it's the reality that counts
Maybe I should start being more jolly
Rather than keep saying
I'm sorry.

Evie Welland (12)
Kingsbury School, Kingsbury

Gone But Not Forgotten

Dark clouds,
Blue skies,
Black rivers,
It reminds me of her.
Whatever happens,
She's always there.

Like blackbirds,
And green fields,
An orchard full of apples,
She will be there.

She will be there when I'm sad,
And when I'm happy,
She was my best friend but now she is gone,
I'm alone,
Worried, scared.
But I know she'll be there,
In my thoughts and in my heart, she is close by.

Bethany Oakley (11)
Kingsbury School, Kingsbury

Imagine Being So Crazy

Imagine being so crazy,
So crazy, you drive people mad,
Mad is another word for crazy,
I'm crazy, are you?
It's okay to be crazy,
I can be crazy too,
Crazy is cool,
Crazy is awesome,
Crazy like a clown,
Clowns are funny,
Clowns make me laugh,
Crazy like a witch,
I like to see witches on Halloween,
I like Halloween, do you?
Crazy is wonderful,
Crazy is beautiful,
Imagine being so crazy.

Eva Sharp (12)
Kingsbury School, Kingsbury

The Ocean

T he symphony of waves in an endless dance
H idden world for us all to explore
E xuberance bubbled inside me

O rcas migrating in the morning light
C oral sitting elegantly capturing the attention of nearby divers
E els burrowing into the sand
A balones feeding on algae, clinging on strong to rocks
N eedlefish making short jumps out of the water, while hunting their prey.

Lily-Rose Pointon (11)
Kingsbury School, Kingsbury

The Weather

The rain came down
Making people frown
The leaves fell down
From the trees to the ground
The kids wish they could play
On the playground

The kids look around
Seeing the rain has died down
The kids walk out
They suddenly hear a sound
Lightning strikes down
The kids run around
They eventually find sheltered ground
They go underneath
And wait for the storm to die down.

Lucy Charlton (13)
Kingsbury School, Kingsbury

A Grieving Soul

A grieving heart sails on a treacherous sea
I cannot comprehend
The pain I fear
Death is such a thief
But life is still precious
I still stand beside you at night
In the darkness of my room
My old friend
Death can't part us from
Our strong, loving bond
You may be gone from my arms
But I still hold you tightly in my heart.

Tegan Carlin (13)
Kingsbury School, Kingsbury

Breaking The Ice

Scraping blades,
Harmonising with quiet music,
The harsh beating of your pumping heart,
Stressful worries vanish in a blink of an eye,
A smile stretches ear to ear,
Each twist, each turn,
A ballerina on blades in a world of ice,
So near, so dear.
Skating alone, round and round the ice rink,
What I came to forget... I forgot.

Immy Brown (12)
Kingsbury School, Kingsbury

What Truth Really Means

The truth is still the truth, even if no one believes it.
A lie is still a lie, even if everyone believes it.
What I know for sure is that speaking your truth is the most powerful tool we have.
I'm for the truth, no matter who tells it.
I'm for justice, no matter who it's for or against.
The truth will set you free!

Kya Baker (11)
Kingsbury School, Kingsbury

Rainbows

Rainbows come into the sky
When the sun and rain are both up high
Rainbows make the dark clouds light
Like an angel in the night
Up in the sky way up high
Up like a star there you are
Always looking down on me
And protecting my family
Rainbows always put a smile on my face
Even when I'm in a sad place.

Olivia Lee-Wilkes (11)
Kingsbury School, Kingsbury

Happiness

Happiness is like the fresh, crisp crunch of freshly fallen leaves,
Like a warm hot chocolate on a cold winter's day.
Happiness is like a nice warm hug on a cold day,
Like a smile on a rainy day,
Like a bonfire on a cold night,
Like spending time with family.

Be kind, and happiness will come to you.

Molly Abbott (12)
Kingsbury School, Kingsbury

Music Is The Key Of Life

Music is the key of life,
It makes you sing and makes you dance.
It turns your frown upside down
And makes you want to shout it out.
It makes the sun always shine, even on a rainy day,
It lifts your spirits, gets them high,
So it gives you something money can't buy.
Music is the key of life.

Alexi-Grace (12)
Kingsbury School, Kingsbury

The New Beginning

School is now here,
A new beginning.
Lots of cheers,
Lots of moans.

People get ready,
For their wonderful start.
They get their supplies,
Ready for school.

Children prepare,
As it's time,
The time for a new beginning.

Evan Foster (11)
Kingsbury School, Kingsbury

Pain

The teardrop rain
Caused my family pain
The bright lightning
Became very frightening
The loud thunder
Made my fish wonder
How a cloud
Could be so loud
How we hoped for some sun
Life could be so fun.

George Moppett (13)
Kingsbury School, Kingsbury

Football

When I hit the ball, my problems fly away;
it's pretty much my therapy.
I have had a lifelong dream to be scouted.
It will happen;
I don't care what anyone says.
I'm making my family proud.

Callum Bryan (11)
Kingsbury School, Kingsbury

Brand New

She was seven when she went on the train for the first time
She sat right up close to the glass window staring out of it
As though she would never experience it again
And, of course, she would never experience it for the first time again
And maybe that was why
Her smile lit up the carriage, contagious
A whole life of train rides ahead of her

She went again when she was eight, babbling about the last time
She didn't feel the need to stare out of the window this time
Instead, she read her book
You see, last time she had no focus
This time she had learnt
She sang songs when the book became too boring
Songs from the last time
And there was a new person on that train
But only slightly new

There was a large gap before she went again
The world was torn apart by illness
But she sat on the train again
Still engrossed in a book
But this time did not look up
She did not sing songs
Or do funny dances

She stayed quiet
Only speaking to ask her mother for water
She did not sit up against the glass this time
But preferred to be in the aisle
And, again, there was a new person on that train
But still only slightly

The next time she was on the train, there was no book in her hands
No paper to write on
Just a small screen
Only just bigger than her hand

The pretty colours would have appealed to the seven-year-old
The words on this screen to the eight-year-old
But only a small dream was inside of her now
And everyone told her it was impossible
So she sat on the train
Watching other people's success
Through a little window into their lives
Dreaming about her own
And there was a new person on that train
Brand new.

Evie Hiscocks (13)
Longsands Academy, St Neots

Greek God Attributes

Apollo, the god of sun and music,
Has the power of health and illness.
Poseidon, the god of the ocean,
Has to give those worthy creativity.

Athena, the goddess of wisdom and war,
Cursed to see her worshippers fall.
Zeus the god of sky and thunder,
Beckons to hear kingdoms call.

Aphrodite, the goddess of beauty and love,
Has a jealous reign from the stars above.
However, Hermes will always be up for fun,
With the wings on his helmet, that son of a gun.

The last on this list is Hephaestus.
He is the god that made all of us.

Lia Fron (12)
Longsands Academy, St Neots

Murder In Paradise

In my eyes and no other,
A wretched beast before me stands,
A contrast to the cherry petals falling from the sky,
Prey, no doubt.

The eyes as deep as the ocean edge,
Tears from the night sky,
Fall as blood spills from this sinful creature,
A sweet aroma fills the air,
Slowly and torturous, as all things alive fall.

Susie Wong (12)
Longsands Academy, St Neots

Untitled

The truth is...

...I won't finish
I won't finish my work at all, at all, yeah, yeah.

I won't finish
I won't finish my work at all, at all, yeah, yeah
Separate work lifts me separately
When this lifting is deep, I won't do
I won't do, yeah, yeah.

All the time when you're rolling with me
I have fun being fidgety
How long are you gonna be with me?
Till we get to the galaxy?
Sneaking out of school just to get by you
I'm obsessed with the work you do
With maths in here and science out there
I hate all the work we do.

But now you just don't listen
You're missin' all my wishes
I'm in maths, but still won't
This work we do is dissing
This is not a maths retreat
I'm playing 'don't play!', it's on repeat
Yeah I'm hoping you see, you see my snap
'Cause I'm not ready for a chicken wrap, whoa!

Jasmine Woolrich (14)
New Skill Centre, Nacton Road

The Beautiful Truth

I own many labels,
Not all of them are pretty,
They don't call me the beautiful girl in a big, bright city,
I own labels I was given, not labels I earned,
Nobody knows my full story,
So how can they name me?
Nobody knows who I am,
Sometimes not even me,
I become multiple into one,
They controlled me with string,
I was on the tip of their thumb,
I fall down a spiral of demons and voices,
Eyes over me,
Sometimes I wish it was a dream,
Once again I go into my mind to escape reality,
My life feels haunted like Halloween,
Holding my breath, I stop to scream,
Walking frozen in time,
I want to be let free,
I want to understand the real me,
Instead of sitting in bed,
Eating ice cream,
What a nice dream.

Lacey Pugh (13)
New Skill Centre, Nacton Road

Parental Truths

Sticks and stones will break my bones
But words will never hurt me
The truth is the words on phones
Will stick forever.

I'm not going to tell you again
That's not my painful truth
The truth is I hear it
Again and again.

Eat your dinner
There are starving children in Africa
The truth is now out there
Although her truth doesn't live by the same rules.

Go ask your father
This is a palaver
The truth is
Your
Truth
Is
Fake.

Macey Bestley (14)
New Skill Centre, Nacton Road

The Truth Of Me

The truth is not as you see me,
The truth is always smiling,
The truth is clever and thoughtful,
The truth is unique and quirky.

The truth is not as you see me,
The truth is supportive and funny,
The truth is growing inside,
The truth is trying to survive.

The truth is not as you see me,
The truth is much darker and deeper,
The truth is frightened to speak,
The truth is afraid to cry.

The truth
Is not me, you see?
Not me at all.

Layla Mann (13)
New Skill Centre, Nacton Road

This Is Me

Azure bright and full of life,
Crystal clear like a glistening diamond,
Reefs as pastel as chalk,
The surface lustrous clear.

A cover of light; dark letters inside,
Bookends of life and death,
My scuffed edges hiding,
A deeper story.

The sea, a stimulant for my brain,
Like a book bland on the outside,
Shallow rays of sunlight pierce through,
Searchlights for greatness and success.

A pristine page.

Aaron L'Argent (13)
New Skill Centre, Nacton Road

The Truth Of My Life

My life
Secondary school, bullied
"Ginger four-eyes"
It's just the way I looked
So angry at times
At the end of my book.
Mum
GP
Off school, back to school
Look out teacher
Off school, back to school
Nobody could reach me
September
New school

Two years to go

Hope
lifts
my
wings.

Zak Fisher (13)
New Skill Centre, Nacton Road

Beautiful Bloom

Thoughtful, cheerful, kind,
Son, brother, grandson, family,
Family is everything to me,
Family blooms inside me.

Daniel Foreman (14)
New Skill Centre, Nacton Road

My Feelings

First thoughts about my feelings.
To be honest, I haven't been truthful to some people.
I lie sometimes and I don't know why.
I don't know why I keep my favourite characters to myself...
I don't know why when I was in year six I was jealous of my best friend.
When I'm at (secondary) school, it feels like I'm being someone else...
Not the true me.
And I keep things to myself from other people.
And I admit I was a bad person at (primary) school.
And I said some hurtful things I regretted and at the time I didn't know the meaning of.

Imogen Ford (12)
Newton Abbot College, Newton Abbot

The Not-So-Beautiful Truth

They tell us,
Our phones are an addiction,
Take them away,
But don't understand the struggle that we face,
Cutting ourselves and suicide,
We're never enough,
These kids in the sky,
Seemed like it was the only way,
But it's a permanent solution,
To a temporary issue,
There may be bad days,
But life will get better,
So don't do it...

Please.

Emmy Scott-Cleasby (12)
Newton Abbot College, Newton Abbot

Drumming

Drumming is a mind of its own,
Bang the drum, you wouldn't want there to be a crack in it.
When you bang it for the first time,
It sends a shock down your spine.
Bang, bang, bang, the drum says.
But when you stop playing, it all goes away,
So take your time with pleasure when you play,
So when you play, do it with joy.

William Neno (11)
Newton Abbot College, Newton Abbot

Our Beautiful Truth

"How would you feel if your armour couldn't protect you?"
I have turned from predator to prey,
No one knows how long we'll stay,
Hiding in the shadows isn't much fun,
It's even worse on the run.
People they come and after they're gone,
Another one of us, disappeared by dawn,
It's hard seeing the ones we love perish,
All because the two-legged are selfish.

"How would you feel if a cage was your safe space?"
A number tag in my ear,
I try to cry but they can't hear,
I'm damaged, I'm broken,
I'm just a pharmaceutical token,
It's not just the cream that makes my eyes burn,
The bright white lights that they turn,
I wonder where the people in the white coats go,
They leave and out goes the bright glow,
It may be lonely stuck in the cage,
But it's better than being front and centre on stage,
(I've heard the rumours.)
Why can't they take my place?

"How would you feel if your commute was a trap?"
I venture every day
Waiting, afraid
The boats don't see us when we swim,
We're less evolved than those with speedy fins,
The journey I take into the unknown,
Very frightening when you're all alone,
My blubber keeps me warm,
It's used for me not for you to form,
What products do you make?
When you don't see the real risk you take,
The life of me or another,
Taken away by a manhunter.

Erin Budd (12)
Oasis Academy Sholing, Sholing

Reflections Through Shattered Glass

Don't read fashion magazines,
They make you feel ugly
With 'perfection' staring back at you
You always need to be:
Pretty and flawless
Petite and beautiful
The 'unrealistic' version of yourself.

The girls in the magazines are the beauty standard
And I am not.
Their faces, the version we aspire to be
And I am not.

Not fat but not skinny,
"Her body fits the mold,"
The one men make.

Who tell me
Mine is always
Too big
Too loose
My face
Too spotty
Too round.

To be pretty
I must be myself
Unique like everybody else,
But to be pretty
I must not be me.

Another version of myself:
Change my hair,
My face,
And my waist.
I must erase what was once there,
Dumb myself down.
Then will they finally like me?
The girls
In the magazines are perfect.

So I try,
Make myself look older -
Cover my face in products to make it look 'better'.

But
I don’t look like myself
I stare in the mirror and
My screen’s reflection.
I wish I could say
That I love the way I look
But I wish I had the hourglass figure:
A body that all the pretty girls have.

I wish I had the frame
That made all the boys
Watch
As I walk away.
But today
I am seen as
Normal rather than beautiful.

Charlotte Stranathan (13)
Oasis Academy Sholing, Sholing

Our Ugly Lies

We're living a lie,
Nature's dying,
And everybody knows why.

Animals deleted,
Giraffes, rhinos, leopards,
Lions and tigers and bears.

Some we can't save,
Fallen angels against the monstrous humans,
Yet we can help those still alive.

It used to be beautiful,
Where every animal roamed the land,
Unafraid of us,
They used to live in peace,
But we ruined that,
But you ruined that.

You ruined it,
With your cars, rubbish, and food,
For your own entertainment,
You imprisoned these animals.

There is so much you could do,
You could save these animals,
But you don't.

Evie Ricketts (14)
Oasis Academy Sholing, Sholing

My Beautiful Brain

Sometimes thinking feels like you can't even try,
Sometimes feeling feels like a cloud of smoke,
Sometimes the scrambled eggs in our head make us feel
Like we are not good enough,
Like I'm repeating myself...
Like I'm repeating myself...
Like...
Wait, I think I've already said that.

As sometimes what our brain says make us feel unworthy,
Makes us feel angry,
Makes us feel sad and happy and all the emotions but
Our insults are lies.
The truth is...
I do say sorry too much,
I get *overexcited*, a lot.
I can't concentrate, often.
But I love this wonderful water in my head, and I always will.
Just because it drowns me sometimes,
Doesn't mean I can't swim.

You see,
There are a lot of people like me,
Who don't find thinking easy,
And overcomplicate simple thoughts like:
How do I do this? or
What is 2x2?

But the thing at the end of the day is,
It is our flaws that make us succeed,
Even though I struggle so much,
I try to think as much as I can and make myself as good as I am,
Doesn't matter how much I can't or I can,
By the end of it all,
You are just as same as I am.

Lara Elliott (12)
Oasis Academy Sholing, Sholing

The Lies You've Told

All the lies you've told,
The fake stories you've recalled
To generations of kids:
Your lies have spread.
Their imagination's now dead
Because of you, and your stupid little head.

You tell them, "Everything's fine"
While you chop off another tree's spine.
You spread your dirty mindsets
To generations to come:
"It's for the better!"
But we're not dumb.

Intoxicating and killing our old Mother Earth
For nothing - just your factory's worth.
Our air now filled with chemicals,
Poison filling our ventricles.
"It's for the better!" you say.
But, oh, you will pay.

You've ruined our kids' futures.
You've ruined our childhoods, our imaginations.
You've spread lies into our minds and lives.
You'll wish that you could go back in time or rewind.

All the homes of our dear animals you have destroyed,
Just so you could be employed.
Just so that you could earn a few bucks.
All the damage you've done without knowing: it really sucks.
All the kids you have hurt, human or not.

All the blood you've made, the innocent spill:
Does it give you a thrill?

Angelika Golabek
Oasis Academy Sholing, Sholing

Worthless Woods, Worthless Words

We are people,
Not ones you can see,
Children of Mother Nature,
Ghosts of what could been.
A tree we are,
A redwood high,
One tree could reach towards the sky,
Yet plundered forward,
Shaken too,
Our insides taken,
Used as glue.
Some worthless scribbles,
Upon our face,
Thrown away without a trace.
Mashed up in 'General Waste'.
I fear we cannot grow,
For they kill to and fro,
Half our species,
Now mounds of ash,
Axes give a fatal lash,
Even now
We cannot sleep,
Used as stools beneath your feet.
Reclaim our worth or use us no more,
Let the trees grow tall.

Lily Hull (12)
Oasis Academy Sholing, Sholing

The Ugly Truth

You want to know the truth right,
Well, we have to help fight,
So this is why I write,
Us as a society have caused this,
But us as a society can change this.

Oxygen's decreasing,
While half the planet's sleeping,
And no, you're not dreaming,
Our planet is overheating.

But we can change our actions,
We can lead the way,
Come on let's create a brighter day.

Cut down on paper or recycle more,
Don't just shut the door,
Put stuff in the bin,
What we are doing is not a sin,
But it will be if we keep littering.

More fumes are released every day,
Try a bus and go the environmental way,
So just use your inner voice,
After all, we need to make the right choice.

Esme Moore (11)
Ormiston Rivers Academy, Burnham-On-Crouch

The Beautiful Truth

Sometimes I feel like,
There is a storm inside my head,
Raindrops crashing down,
And dark clouds lurking above.

Silhouettes of human-like trees,
Grab onto me, luring me in,
Whilst deafening thoughts and cries,
Surround my head.

No light is seen,
No stars fill the sky,
Neither does the hiding moon,
No lantern in hand, I walk in the dark.

Loud silence is all the ears can hear,
No creature is stirring,
No footsteps are heard,
Only my echoing thunder-like thoughts.

Shivering in fear,
I walk on the path,
I go past puddles, watching my reflection,
And then I think.

Who is hiding?
Who is behind those murky eyes?
Who is behind that window,
That peers into my soul?

I look inside and see a girl,
A smiling, laughing, dancing girl,
Sun rays beam onto her glass-like skin,
Her smile reaching her glimmering eyes.

Jealousy fills up the empty space inside me,
I wish I could be like her, I think,
She is having a great time,
Not a cloud surrounds her,
Not a worry in sight.

Suddenly, the rain stops,
I look around,
It is still dark,
But the storm has vanished.

Then something washes over me,
Like a tidal wave,
Can I?
Should I?

Yes. I should.

I break through the wet window,
Glass shattering all over the floor,
With a deep breath,

I jump in.

A huge, snow-covered mountain,
Jumps up in front of me,
I look around,
But all I can see is the mountain and a plain field.

Nowhere else to go,
I hesitantly start trekking,
Trekking up the rock giant,
For a moment, I see the girl...

I walk up the mountain,
I freeze like a statue,
Next to me, and all the way up,
Are people.

Then I realise,
These aren't just people,
They're memories,
They're my mistakes.

The times when I said something wrong,
Did something terrible,
Judged somebody,
All the mistakes I put behind me, not caring.

Once I get to the peak of the mountain,
And overlook the fields,
It comes to me,
I suddenly realise.

All the mistakes I made,
I put at the back of my mind,
Not even thinking of the damage,
I have done.

I haven't been my true self,
I haven't been the truth,
What have I done?
I have been such a goof!

So I learn from my mistakes,
I get up and try,
No matter the weather,
Sunshine or storm.

I push the clouds away,
And erase the rain,
Flowers bloom,
And my true colours inside of me,
Have exploded in joy.

So I may give a message to everyone out there:
Climb the mountain.
Sail across the sea.
You will reach your dreams.
Only if you try,

You will find the beautiful truth.

Jess Hatton (11)
Ormiston Rivers Academy, Burnham-On-Crouch

Beautiful

Beautiful, that is what you are,
Beautiful, that is the truth,
Beautiful, that is what most of us think we have to be,

The time I felt truly free is when the world stopped for me,
I believe, that is what I say,
To cheer me up on a rainy day,

The world needs to change before it is gone,
If it doesn't, life will go wrong,
Life is like a game of ping-pong,
You can start again,

I'm unique because I say I am,
But is it enough, when I believe I can,
The world won't change,
But you can,

I am angry about all the things we have done wrong
But so is everyone young and old,
Anger doesn't change anything, no matter what,

The memory that haunts me is one that's old,
It never changes as it unfolds,
In my mind I'm full of doubts,
But it is really full of clout,

The real me is one that doesn't show,
But then again none of ours do,
In my dreams I try to imagine a world without problems,
But then, it wouldn't be beautiful, because it wouldn't be the truth,

The truth is beautiful, and that's a fact,
The truth is beautiful,
Let's leave it at that.

Zhani Green (11)
Ormiston Rivers Academy, Burnham-On-Crouch

Be The Reason There Is A Next Generation

In a world where sirens are loud and young people's voices are quiet,
And the sound of fresh running water is ruined by the falling climate,
In a world where car engines roaring are louder than the birds fluttering in the sky,
Our world is falling apart and I wonder why.

Not because of this generation,
But because of inflation,
Because of discrimination,
Because of inequality in education,
The list goes on,
And we've been told it was our fault since the moment we were born.

So let's make a change,
Let's make the old people look at us strange,
We will show them they're wrong,
We will show them we are not the problem and the list goes on and on,
The old people say that they can fix it,
But I think it's up to us to win it.

They say that they understand the urgency,
But if they actually did they would know it's not a little problem, it's an emergency,
I can do this, we can do this as a team,
But we need to hurry up before more animals start to scream,
So let's stand as a nation,
And be the reason that there is a next generation.

Niamh Phillips (11)
Ormiston Rivers Academy, Burnham-On-Crouch

Bound By Love, Freed By Hate

If you love something, let it go,
If you hate something, learn to grow.
'Cause roses have their thorns
And snakes must shed to be reborn.

The truth is not always pretty,
Hatred is what makes us blind.
'Cause some people believe the things
They hear for the first time.

Love brings power, trust and belief,
But it makes you scared and
Vulnerable to deceit.

In every scar, a story unfolds,
Beauty lies where the truth is told.
Through the struggle, our hearts learn to see
That even brokenness can set us free.

In the fire of hate, we find strength to break free,
While love can ensnare us, binding us with fear's decree.
Through trials and turmoil, our hearts learn to see,
From bitter struggles, I find the beautiful truth in me.

April Fowler (12)
Ormiston Rivers Academy, Burnham-On-Crouch

Equality Is But A Figment Of Imagination

I am angry, so angry
The poor are suffering and for what?
For the rich to take their efforts and label them as their own
For the time they spent in vain
Why is this world so unbalanced?
Why is this world so unfair?

I am sad, so sad
People are dying, for what?
For nothing
For their cries for help are ignored
I am sad
Sad that these people are invisible
In stories, people steal money
Real life is not so different but the money we are trading is instead lives.
Why is no one taking action?

Evie Pearse (11) & Grace Fox (12)
Ormiston Rivers Academy, Burnham-On-Crouch

Why Am I Not Good Enough?

Why am I not good enough?
Why don't I fit in?
Why do I act so differently?
Why am I so weird?

Why do I feel so stupid?
Why do I mess everything up?
But I look at you
And you are good enough
You fit in and you are not different and you are not weird
You are not stupid and you don't mess things up
Everyone loves you and you are never alone

But maybe you do feel stupid
And maybe you do feel alone
Maybe you think that you are different or that everyone hates you
Or maybe you're hiding it all

So if you do feel this way
You are not the only one
There are others just like you
And others just like me
So I'm telling you now that you are perfect
Just the way you are.

Katherine Heathcote (13)
Ryecroft CE Middle School, Rocester

My Passion: Mountain Biking

M TB
O ver the bars
U ltimate danger
N erves kick in
T ackle the terrain
A drenaline punch
I am crazy
N o fear

B rakes, don't
I t's fun
K ey to biking
I gnore slow-down signs
N earby trails
G ain confidence

A crazy world
D irt on my helmet
R ough terrain
E nter the world of biking
N ervous
A crazy trail
L oaded ride
I ncorrect technique
N o brakes
E dge of the *drop.*

Sid Yeomans (11)
Ryecroft CE Middle School, Rocester

Oh How The World Goes By

A lion's roar reverberates through the craft
My thin, pale hand trembles
Adrenaline courses through my fragile bones
Those muddy, sparse fields that failed my family
The dilapidated cobblestone that I used to call home
The rolling hills gaze at me
Almost regretfully
But I don't care
I'm gliding through velvety soft clouds
Dancing away from every fear and charging towards my hopes and dreams
The world is racing by, radiating a sense of freedom
Everything is so green and so fresh
A warmth engulfs me
Life is not a hardship
It is a joy.

Fraser Pickup (13)
Ryecroft CE Middle School, Rocester

My Feelings

Sometimes I'm sad
Sometimes I'm angry
Sometimes I'm worried
Sometimes I'm scared
But when I feel these emotions
I think about all the beautiful things
I think about my pet dog
I think about my friends
I think about art
I think about Lego
I think about my family
I think about my home
I think about a hot day at the beach
I think about our galaxy and all the planets inside
I think about reading
I think about music
And after I think about all these things
I no longer feel sad or angry
All I feel is happiness.

Emilia Gill (11)
Ryecroft CE Middle School, Rocester

My Sister's Brain Has Been Switched With A Fly's

Once she was smart
She was intelligent
She excelled at art
Was even good at maths
But now it seems all she does is fart

She was almost as smart as a dolphin
When the brain switching began
But that was long ago
Back when she ran

Because gradually
Week by week, day by day
She kept switching brains
And now it seems like all she does is play

It started in Year Four and ever since
She visited doctors even scientists
But all the stupidity we tried to rinse
Stayed with her and won't ever leave.

Amelia Walsham (11)
Ryecroft CE Middle School, Rocester

My Emotions

Sometimes I'm sad
Sometimes I'm mad
But when I am either of these
I try to forget and laugh
I think about the birds that are high in the sky
I think about how easy it is for them to fly
Sometimes I'm happy
Sometimes I'm excited
But I don't do anything about it
I just giggle and grin
I think about the things that make me smile
And dump them into a great big pile
Sometimes I'm embarrassed
Sometimes I'm anxious
But I don't like feeling like this
Not at all, not even a little bit.

Scarlett Salt (12)
Ryecroft CE Middle School, Rocester

Memories

That smell, can you smell it?
I can - it's the smell of memories.
Memories that bring back the beautiful truth,
The truth I love.
The smell is sending me back, back to the times that I want to remember.

Right now, I remember - I remember the times when I was young.
Right now, I remember - I remember being small.
Right now, I remember - I remember the beautiful truth.

I want to sit here all day, all night,
But I can't because
I have remembered I have more of my beautiful life
To enjoy.

Sophia Plant (12)
Ryecroft CE Middle School, Rocester

The Team For Me

From the staggering stands of Pride Park Stadium,
And the roar of the crowd.
I've seen us go up,
I've seen us go down.
All of the chants rattling my brain.

Steve Bloomer's watching,
Helping the fight.
Derby County fans,
We bleed black and white.
Formed in 1884,
120 years before I was born.

Proud member of the founding twelve,
Kevin Hector, Roy McFarland, Craig Bryson,
All putting trophies on our shelves.
Thank you again, DCFC,
As you are the team for me.

Finley Baron (13)
Ryecroft CE Middle School, Rocester

The Aliens Are Real

Walking through the field
The moon like a diamond
Emerging from the forest
Then I saw it
The bright blue beam shone down from
A flying pod
What is it?
Am I going crazy?
The little green man waved
So I waved back
The blue beam began pulling up animals
What do I do?
It was blazing, closer and closer
Sucking them up
Like a vacuum cleaner
Well, I managed to escape
And I've never told anyone til this day
What do I do now?

Frankie Gaunt-Bott (12)
Ryecroft CE Middle School, Rocester

Batman Begins

A Gotham night, quite the fright
In the shadows, waiting to catch the Joker and his crew in the act
Not so fast, people to save with Alfred in the Bat Cave

The Joker arose, not scared at all
Pinned to the wall, grinning at them all

Batman is here - there's no need to fear
Quite the cheer
Batman's in gear

Riddle me this, quite the twist
Riddle me this
What comes up but never goes down?
You'll never know, now you have a big frown!

Parker Venables (12)
Ryecroft CE Middle School, Rocester

Peaceful Life

The fiery sun rises again
As my eyes open
The day starts
I chase my friend around the kitchen
The cat
Whilst I run as fast as I can
Breakfast is ready
A peaceful morning with lots of attention and the love of my owners
Then they leave for work
Deep concentration as I lay eyes on the old cat
I'm chasing the cat around again
Afternoon nap, here I come
I wake up and my loving owners arrive
Love, attention and most of all kindness
I love life.

Chloe Sessions (12)
Ryecroft CE Middle School, Rocester

Thoughts And Feelings

I am small but creative
I am religious but a kid
I am a gymnast and also a dancer
While I'm all these things, I'm also me.

I like English but not reading
I like Disney but I'm not a thrill-seeker
I like giving but not taking
Whatever I like or hate, I am perfect.

I hope to be a teacher, but not with older kids
I hope to get a sausage dog but not a sausage roll
I hope to go to Paris
But, while I have hopes, I also have feelings.

Sophie Bembridge (11)
Ryecroft CE Middle School, Rocester

I Am Myself

This is me:

Sister
Annoying, fierce
Caring, farmer, helpful
Confident, tractors, cows, football
Sports, friends, family
Energetic, loud

I am myself.

Georgia Palmer (11)
Ryecroft CE Middle School, Rocester

The Dragodon

Time on this island
Time here fixes everything
Wound healing
Trees rotting after falling
But how quickly they say 'it' holds time, but does it?
Yes, 'it' does, as the legends say
A benevolent being, bigger than a caver, bigger than the oil rig out at sea
The beast from our worst nightmares
The dragodon
Humanity will now face the consequences of using weapons
'It' sleeps until
Now!

William Stringer (11)
Ryecroft CE Middle School, Rocester

Childhood

Your life is different to mine
Especially your childhood
Some grow up blissful
Some want to grow up already
But why?
Why?
Why?
Oh why?
Why didn't you pick your family?
Your place to live?
You chose the life of someone else
And not yourself
The impact you made
Was not for the better
But now that will have to do
You can't buy that back now
We're all grown up.

Evah Millen (12)
Ryecroft CE Middle School, Rocester

That One Sneeze

You can feel your nose tingling
Head tilted back
You feel the sneeze riling up in your nose
Your hands cupped in front of your face, ready to catch the sneeze
Your eyes start to water at the need to let it out
Then all of a sudden
The sneeze just goes
You feel annoyed that you stopped what you were doing just to sneeze and yet you never did
It just poofed, and disappeared like a rabbit running from its prey.

Emily Moore (12)
Ryecroft CE Middle School, Rocester

Aliens Rule

Humans - oh, I despise them, thinking they're so good with their money and transportation
Aliens are just better - we've built everything from scrap metal
We're smarter than humans who are lazy, oh so lazy
And we've planned to destroy Earth for thousands of years but we've never got away with it
Aliens deserve the Earth, humans deserve nothing
It's time for us to rule them out!

James Bosworth (12)
Ryecroft CE Middle School, Rocester

Truth, Honesty, Power

Truth, honesty, power
Those are the things that lie in your hands
You have the truth
You have the power
You have the reason to be honest

Truth, honesty, power
Your hands hold memories
Your hands hold reasons
Your hands are unique

Truth, honesty, power
You are beautiful
So, don't let people discourage you
The world won't be the same without you.

Darcie Van Der Westhuizen (11)
Ryecroft CE Middle School, Rocester

Me, Myself And I

I am as private as a coconut
I am as cool as ice cream
I am as sweet as jelly
I am as salty as McDonald's chips
I am as tall as a tree
I am as sour as a lemon
I am as sly as a fox
I am as competitive as a football player
I am a banana
I am as yellow as a pineapple
I am different inside like a watermelon
I am me
I am who I want to be.

William Walker (11)
Ryecroft CE Middle School, Rocester

An Oasis Tribute

A tribute to Noel and Liam Gallagher.

Someday you will find me
Caught beneath the landslide
But where were you when we were imprecise

Nobody knows the way it's gonna be
'Cause all of the stars are fading away
Just try not to worry
Stop crying your heart out

You and I are gonna live forever
Little by little
I know I'm leaving but I'll be back another day.

Zak Barker (12)
Ryecroft CE Middle School, Rocester

I Am...

I am short, but inside I am tall
I am an enemy, but inside I am a friend
I am a fighter, but inside I love
Labels on the outside can be true
But the real things that count are inside.

I like car culture, but I also love bikes
I like F1, but I will always take a hike
My truth can be anything that I like
But it hides down below.

Jayden Bowd (12)
Ryecroft CE Middle School, Rocester

I'm A Potato

I'm a potato
Darkness
Dirt
All I see is dirt
All I hear is, well, dirt
Waiting
Waiting
Is all
I ever
Do
Waiting to be picked among
The rows and rows of potatoes just like me and you
Well, maybe not you because you're cool
Do you want to know why?
It's because I am a potato.

Christopher Heathcote (11)
Ryecroft CE Middle School, Rocester

Cows

Cows are beautiful things
All in different breeds
Some small, some tall
Some with colours, some white
Playing and bouncing around bright green fields
Chewing on juicy grass and pink flowers
Rolling around in mud
Lying down in the summer sun
Brown, white, black, spotty or fluffy
Cows are beautiful things.

Phoebe Bond (11)
Ryecroft CE Middle School, Rocester

My Brother's Hilarious

My brother's hilarious.
He keeps on laughing when
Nothing is making him laugh.
He laughs and laughs.
He warms people's hearts, even
me, the person who is writing.
What's his name? I hear you cry.
Well, his nickname is Beany,
And my mum gave it to him
When he was the size of a jellybean.

Harry Jarvis (12)
Ryecroft CE Middle School, Rocester

Scouts Because Of You

Camping, fires, first aid
Things Scouts can do together
Hiking, socials, sports

Because of you
She can do first aid

Because of you
She can do rock climbing

Because of you
She can camp in the world

Because of you
She is a Girl Scout who can follow the rules.

Millie Lewis (13)
Ryecroft CE Middle School, Rocester

It

It knows everything about you
It'll never leave your side
Its chainsaw hums in the depths of night
It looks at you through windows
Who knows, it could be with you while you're reading this.
It giggles at night
And whispers through pipes
Be careful
It's with you
Run.

Corinne Metcalfe (11)
Ryecroft CE Middle School, Rocester

You

Humans are growers, yet destroyers
Heartless, yet kind
Strong, yet weak
The same, yet different
Courageous, yet cowardly
Intelligent, yet clueless.

Be the real you in a world that doesn't want you to be
Be the rebel
Be the change
Be your own beautiful truth.

Matilda Cartwright (11)
Ryecroft CE Middle School, Rocester

Me

F irst means nothing to me.
R est is everything you need.
E veryone is welcome.
D eath is nothing to me at all.
D oom will come, I will be ready.
I t will never, ever end me.
E veryone is themselves.

Freddie Sandall (11)
Ryecroft CE Middle School, Rocester

A Single Fish

Just me, myself and I
Dodging all the spiky rods
It's like we're playing hide-and-seek
Trying to make some friends
But they all disappear
I'm too small
I'm trapped in clear blue water
Swimming on and on and on.

Romaysae Terbaoui (11)
Ryecroft CE Middle School, Rocester

Untitled

One glance sends it flowing through the veins
Now it's three in the morning
Shop like a robot from 1984
Going past the 505
Cold monkeys from Sheffield.

Jacob Udale (12)
Ryecroft CE Middle School, Rocester

Perspective Beauty

Perspective, beauty
I want a community
Filled with chaotic unity
One with people that
Understand life is not flat
Like a coin
But something joined
Made of many faces
From many places
A beautiful world, a beautiful community
Is one filled with people without discontinuity

I want a family
That I hold avidly
Our best traits
Aren't always straight
Give us our freedom
My parents gave me a great sum
I would build up a house
With children, me and my spouse
A beautiful home, a beautiful family
Is one built around emotional gravity

I want a job
One that won't make me sob
A daily occurrence
That makes a difference
In my life, in your life
To try and erase recent strife
Entertainment for many
Public joy available in plenty
A craftsman, a playwright
Could I really do this right?
A beautiful role, a beautiful job
Is one that could never be swapped

I want a life
With the excitement of a dive
With a community
Built through my people's unity
A place to raise my family
Which they watch avidly
Where I can do my job
Which would bring smiles and sobs
A beautiful truth, a beautiful life
A perfect imperfection that fits my type.

Neel Aswani (15)
Samuel Ryder Academy, St Albans

Flowers 3

Some are used to poison
Some are used to heal

Some are used as gifts
Others are used to kill

Some are used for their beauty
Some are used for their smell

Some are often admired
Others are often shunned

Some are left to grow wild
Others are kept neat in pots

Some are meant to eat
Some are meant to be eaten

Some are meant to be picked
Others are meant to prick
The meaning of a flower is often changed
In the way they are carefully arranged

Right hand, left hand
The colour of the ribbon to the colour of the vase.

The number of flowers,
To their colour and shape.

Red roses symbolise romantic passion
Whilst yellow roses can symbolise rejection

Poppies symbolise death
Dandelions often symbolise freedom

Marigolds symbolise grief
Nightshades symbolise danger

Daffodils symbolise joy
Petunias symbolise anger,

A complicated language of secrecy
In the high expectation within Victorian society
I will never stop thanking Allah
For the lovely creation of flowers.

As flowers are used to talk the truth
Amongst a world of silence.

Sanaa Berhili (13)
Samuel Ryder Academy, St Albans

The Beautiful Truth

Our world is beautiful
Green and wild
Our culture is beautiful
Vibrant and unique
Humans are beautiful

If this land is so great, then why do we ruin it?
We litter and pollute
We destroy and burn
This isn't how it should be
This world is fake

Our culture is wonderful, yet we fight about it
We start wars and we kill
We fight and we battle
This isn't how it should be
This world is fake

We are ruining our world
What used to be thriving
Is now dying
How does that make you feel?
The beautiful truth is being lost

Sea levels are rising
Ice is melting
Our planet is warming
Can't you see that we're not helping?

Humans take, humans thieve
We turn our world from grey to steel
We kill creatures every day
Sometimes I think we've forgotten how to feel

Don't you miss those quiet places?
No noise, just peace
Sometimes now they're hard to find
As humans take what nature designed

We are ruining our world
What used to be thriving
Is now dying
How does that make you feel?
The beautiful truth is being lost.

Evie Tomasi (13)
Samuel Ryder Academy, St Albans

The Beautiful Truth

The Beautiful Truth
Is one that takes courage
To leave my lips
And touch your heart.

The Beautiful Truth
Is that your hair looks nice today
That I love how your eyes shimmer in the sunlight
That I'm proud of you, for just getting out of bed today.

The Beautiful Truth
Is that you're strong – even if you don't know it
That I wish I were you in the ways that you wish you were me
That I love you.

The Beautiful Truth
Is that you should never be jealous
Is that people would kill to be you
To be in your skin, thinking your thoughts.

The Beautiful Truth
Is that I want you
Intoxicating, addictive, lethal
I. Need. You. Too. Much.

The Beautiful Truth
Isn't that beautiful; not to me
Because your beauty kills me
Everything about you kills me.

Honestly?
I wish I could get over you
For your sanity and mine
But your hair does look nice today.

Aimee Baker-Lawrence (14)
Samuel Ryder Academy, St Albans

Untitled

Click! A photo is taken
Flash! Unwarped, untouched
Freeze! Set in stone
Now I will never have to forget

The crinkle of my nose
The sparkle in our eyes
The joy on our faces
The way your hair blew in the wind

All my favourite memories
Moments of fun and laughter
The times I wish never to forget
The memories I want to keep

Forever in my heart
To cherish along with my most prized possessions
My loved ones and ones I hold dearly
Old and new, big and small

So now we live
Along with the rest of the photos
Stored in a penny-sized SD card
And in a photo on my wall

Stored along with all the hundreds of others
All captured with the same single snap
All as beautiful as the ones that came before
And all the ones that will follow

All the complete utter truth
Unwarped, untouched, set in stone.

Lexie Bignell (15)
Samuel Ryder Academy, St Albans

The Beautiful Truth

In the whispers of the dawn's embrace,
The beautiful truth finds its place,
In the laughter of children, pure and bright,
In the stars that shimmer throughout the night.

It dances in the leaves of the ancient trees,
In the gentle hum of the summer breeze,
A tapestry woven with a sacred space.

Through trials and shadows, it shines so clear,
It's the bonds of love that we hold dear,
A reminder that beauty lies within,
In every heart, where the truth begins.

In the eyes of the weary, a spark still glows,
In the stories of struggle, resilience shows,
It whispers in moments both tender and tough,
The beautiful truth is often enough.

Tanisha Sheikh (14)
Samuel Ryder Academy, St Albans

Forgiveness

When it feels like they hurt you, which they probably did,
It may seem hard, but you should forgive.
I know you're waiting for an apology that will never come,
For closure,
But that's not the only way to move on.

Forgive them for their actions and keep going on with your life,
Like the old saying 'forgive and forget', except with a tweak,
Don't forget what they did or you will fall into the same trap again,
But still forgive.

Forgiveness feels like a weight lifted off your chest, off your shoulders,
So you can finally stand straight and breathe,
Be the bigger person since they cannot.

Forgive and closure will follow.

Viola Dominici (15)
Samuel Ryder Academy, St Albans

The Beautiful Truth

In my eyes, everything's beautiful
In my eyes, nothing can be ugly
I wish everybody could see the world as I see it
I know many people would disagree with me
But this is me
In my eyes, everything's beautiful
The way people walk
The way people talk
I know that many people would disagree with me
But this is me
This is me expressing myself
This is me trying to write a poem
And to round this all off I want you to take something away from this poem
You as the reader
You as you
You as the beautiful person
I know you are.

The beautiful truth.

Sylvie Tomasi (11)
Samuel Ryder Academy, St Albans

The Beautiful Truth

In laughter of friends,
In the midst of flowers so bright,
The beautiful truth gleams,
A beacon of light.
With every sigh the night echoes so clear,
A friendship ready to blossom is so near,
The beautiful truth is as pure as a dove,
Held in the warmth of a hand,
Couture as a glove.
For light has a home in our hearts,
Don't ever let your spark of honesty depart,
For the beautiful truth is a wisp of hope,
Let our serene spirits soar,
Together being the antidote.

Aaruthiya Renugoban (12)
Samuel Ryder Academy, St Albans

The Beautiful Truth

The beautiful truth, innocent and kind,
Nowadays it's so hard to find.

The beautiful truth, pure and blind,
Easily manipulated twisted and mined.

The beautiful truth, a work of art,
A masterpiece that touches the heart.

The beautiful truth, a symphony of joy and pain,
A dance of life where love remains.

The beautiful truth, calms the soul,
Once again making it whole.

Jasmine Willis (11)
Samuel Ryder Academy, St Albans

Unveiling The Real

In a world where people wear a mask,
It's hard to find the truth, a big task.
But being real is what we need,
To show our hearts and let them lead.

When we speak and share what's true,
We find real friends, like me and you.
In the noise, let's sing our song,
Being ourselves is where we belong.

Amelia Sieradzka (11)
Samuel Ryder Academy, St Albans

In The Graveyard

In the graveyard where shadows dance,
Nature's beauty takes its chance.
Amidst the tombstones flowers bloom,
Whispering tales of life's brief gloom.

The trees stand tall, their branches sway,
A gentle breeze carries thoughts away.
Birds singing melodies, sweet and clear,
Reminding us life's end draws near.

Though death may cast its solemn shade,
Nature's beauty will never fade,
In the circle of life, we always find,
A reminder to cherish every kind.

So let's embrace both life and death,
In nature's embrace, take a breath.
For in the graveyard's sombre grace,
We find beauty in every place.

Annalise Hyde (15)
Sirius Academy West, Hull

In This Air

In this air, all I hear
Is the sound of cars
protruding in my ear.

The buses rolling,
The vans running
and the rides at Hull Fair, ready to get going.

In this cold winter air
I have a slight cough;
maybe I'll go home and eat some pumpkin broth.

'Tis the time of the year where we cuddle up warm
and stay up late, like it's the norm.
Then we wake up, clueless, at dawn.

Winter is near, and times are cold.
Sometime soon we will forget all this and become old.

Orlan Coulman (12)
Sirius Academy West, Hull

Don't Fear Us

Darkness fills the midnight air with tension,
Lanterns rattle and torches flicker, silence splits the sky,
Cold whips of freezing air and wisps of crisp flames,
They're coming...

Fluffy white clouds drift in the breeze,
Warm rays of sunlight cover the surface of everything around,
Illuminating an orange glow everywhere,
We are ready...

Shaking hands and wobbling knees,
Shadows snake through the air,
Screams fracture the ether,
Help us...

Every noise catches our attention,
Something is lurking nearby,
Below the emerald depths of bushes,
It's here...

Zoey Manning (11)
Soham Village College, Soham

I Am The Mountain

I am the mountain, brave and tall,
I stand blanketed in thick, heavy snow,
I tower over all life like a giant protecting its kingdom,
But it's different now, monsters stalk my peaceful paradise,
Plastics and chemicals drain the beauty from my oceans and seas,
Clouds of ash and smoke poison my dreamy blue skies,
I long to see trees of bright emerald green,
And vibrant flowers the colours of joy once more before it's all gone,
My animals are starving and my plants are dying,
My world's bright spark has gone out,
What beasts could do such a thing?

Isidora Abbott (11)
Soham Village College, Soham

Trees Are Dying

A haiku

Trees are on fire
Their screams around the forest
They are burning fast.

Evelyn Turton (11)
Soham Village College, Soham

For Future Generations

Hello all future generations, I call you all here,
Let's save the world before it will disappear.
The world is dying, and nobody cares,
Or maybe it is because nobody is aware?
Well, we will make them know. And know it shall be so,
Quick, before it all will go.
The Earth is warmer, ice in the Arctic is melting,
Yet barely anyone is even helping.
Do you not even care about the seas, bees or trees?
You cut up trees and the land, say it is progress just for money?
Or would you rather have the sweet taste of honey?
When the pandemic came around, we all had to flee,
And the Earth sighed out heavily with glee.
Without people destroying the land, it just grew,
Some call this fake, but others know it is true.
Someone once said, "The world will soon die."
And that makes many want to cry.
Everything has to die, that is life.
But the way we are doing it, is like stabbing somebody with a knife.
The world is dying and nobody cares,
If we do not save it, it will end in despair.

Wanda Vitkova (11)
St Thomas More RC School, Blaydon-On-Tyne

Life Is What It Is

It's hard
When you're not fully developed
To wake up in the off-season
At 6am
To train and work out
Knowing that all your friends
Are sleeping in
And are laughing with their families.

It's hard
To throw, catch, block, tackle and intercept
And hit others who are way bigger
And way more developed than you
Only to go home that night
Bruised, battered, strained, defeated
But knowing you have to show up again
To face those big guys the next day
For just the chance to try again.

But understand this
When you don't labour yourself, your friends will
And when you fall too deep in the sandbags under your eyes
They'll leave you
They will leave you
They'll leave you skin and bone, bloody and tears
And with a broken heart
And while you weep for those who were supposed to be

Your friends for life
They'll be partying
Not giving two thoughts about you
While they are living life at its peak
You're having yours at its lowest
With those sandbags weighing you down
You think you're defeated
When you turn to your family
The 'so-called' eternal supportives
Looking up and down at your undeveloped self

They push you away
They deny they ever had you
They never wanted you

Knowing that you have no one to look up to
You begin to close in on yourself
Entering depression
Echoes of previous insults inhabit your mind
Stationary in this state for months.

You receive a text from your old school friend, Henry
You and him grab a cuppa
For old time's sake

He stares
Appalled at you
His old, middle-school friend
Transformed into this

Old
Ugly
Chap

You look at him
All dazzling
Even with a suit on!
As he leaves
You uplift your mind
You exterminate the remains of your toxic friends
You smash your stone heart
And you live life once more

You get yourself a high-paying occupation
Lose your hallucination
You begin to work out
Make yourself heard
Your friends are coming back
They all say they want a re-do
They heard you're doing well
You're telling them you can't go back
You won't be alone forever.

Tuka Al-Hafidh (11)
St Thomas More RC School, Blaydon-On-Tyne

The Beautiful Truth

Why can't we all be honest and truthful
As it sets us free.
Instead of hiding behind lies
And misery.

The thing about truth is
It can be denied.
But it leaves a scar
And guilt fills you inside.

When you lie, it can make you
Feel like you are flying
It can make you feel free
But then it stops fortifying.

Then you are remorseful
Here comes honesty, and the burden is gone
You can go back to your life
And time goes back on.

Why can't we all just be truthful and honest?
It should be what we are entitled to
And even promised.

Behind the dishonesty and all the lies.
The beautiful truth still remains inside.

David Adeoye (11)
St Thomas More RC School, Blaydon-On-Tyne

The Ancient Thief

Long ago, when the world was fresh,
Millenniums ago from today,
Everyone was at peace,
There were no fights,
Perfection stayed.

But where there is good, there is always bad,
A shadow in the light,
This particular thief is called Time,
And Time is like a knife.

In the darkness it struck,
Slow but persistent,
It never gave up on its prey,
Year after year, the flowers all wilted,
Even the mountains crumbled in decay.

Flash back to the future, 2024,
Time still wanders the streets,
Stealing the kings and queens of old and new,
This thief didn't miss a beat.

So, when an adult says, "I wish that I had more time!"
I hope this poem comes back to you,
And flashes in your mind.

Just remember that Time is persistent,
It will never stop,
Even after you have died,
And you can't run from Time,
Just like you can't run from Death,
Because eventually...
You'll,
Run,
Out,
Of,
Breath.

Yusuff Hilmi (11)
St Thomas More RC School, Blaydon-On-Tyne

One Billion Years Ago

Sometimes I sit and wonder,
About the things I'll never know,
Like what the world was really like,
One billion years ago.

Did super ants rule the world?
Was the king a giant flamingo?
I wish I knew what the tale was,
One billion years ago.

Did cavemen ride on dinosaurs?
Could a lion jump over a rainbow?
I can only guess what the world was like,
One billion years ago.

We haven't got much evidence,
There's only so much history has to show,
But what was the true picture,
One billion years ago?

It might always stay an unsolved mystery,
We may never see into that shadow,
Of what the world was really like,
One billion years ago.

Luke Rosa (11)
St Thomas More RC School, Blaydon-On-Tyne

Who Knows?

Will the trees disappear?
Will the animals dying in wildfires cause a tear?
Will the wars destroy buildings?
Will the endangered families cry because of mass killings?
Will the seas dry up?
Will the poor have no water to fill their cup?
Will there be no food to feed the mouths of many?
Will the world become uninhabitable, not fit for any?
Will there be another planet for when the Earth is ending?
Will the world go grey and be beyond mending?
Who knows what will happen?
Who knows?

Louie Kerr (12)
St Thomas More RC School, Blaydon-On-Tyne

The Truth

I say the world's melting
They say no one's there
But really I know
That nobody cares.

They say they're trying
They say it's their best
Why is this crisis
Not coming to rest?

Then there goes the coal
The oil could be next
They're saying the right things
They're doing their best.

Our world of black
Is beginning to lighten
Although I'm in pain
I'm no longer frightened.

Amie Watson (11)
St Thomas More RC School, Blaydon-On-Tyne

Truth

A truth is a truth no matter its disguise,
It cannot dwell with secrets, nor with lies.
It is spoken, heard and spoken again,
But it is very rarely written with a pen.
For all of those too scared to speak,
Some call them wise,
Others call them meek.
They all have one thing in common,
All are sad and solemn,
For they live without the truth we speak,
And truth is the way, the light,
It is not meek.

Evie Davidson (11)
St Thomas More RC School, Blaydon-On-Tyne

Faces

One, put the mask on
The curtains open, velvet red, shimmering
Golden ties. There are people, too many, too few
All staring.
Staring at you.
Lift your chin, smile more, all teeth.

Take notes: what colour are their eyes? Don't look
Too close.
Introduce yourself, bow, hand on heart; be sincere
Tell them nothing, don't lie.
Keep the mask securely in place. Start the show.
They will all love you.

Two. Soften your grip.
The curtains close, velvet black, dull
Invisible ties. There are no people, emptiness,
No eyes. The embrace of the familiar.
Relax your eyes, unclench your jaw, take a deep breath.
Colours you know, don't look away.
Laugh, genuine. Smile like you mean it.
Speak, sing, be real. Be you.
Don't lie.
The cracks begin to show, the shadows cut deep.
The show is over.
They all loved you.

Three. Take the mask off.
There are no curtains, jet-black, vacant
Invisible smiles. The theatre is empty,
No eyes. Comfortable numbness, familiar.
You have no eyes, you cannot speak, you cannot breathe.
No sight, no sound, no air. Not of theirs
But your own thoughts.
No colours, Vantablack, closed eyes.
Sudden feeling, sharp sting, like needles or knives.
Cold feeling. Be honest. Don't lie.
There is no more mask,
The shattered remains that lie at your feet.

Tragic, poetic beauty.
The show ended a while ago.
They all loved you.

Marci Ehsan (15)
The George Eliot Academy, Caldwell

Being Fake In A Fake World!

Being fake in a fake world.
It's not who you are.
But you could become
Someone else.

Feel free to let your emotions
Loose, it's only natural, don't hide.
Don't run, because you are already
Where you need to be.

Even knowing that there is
Something else, know you are
Never alone, no matter how you
Feel, or the current situation.

You have abilities, no one could ever
Imagine replicating, because you are
The only you. But if you're
Not happy, take inspiration.

Take inspiration using your
Ears, to listen to the advice
You may need to. Use your
Mouth, to ask for help.

This is for people who are lost,
Who are stuck. Don't be duplicitous.
Don't lie if you need it. Even if you're
Old or young, it does not matter.

Life is tough
But you'll
All be okay.
Just know that.

The world is very weird.
It's real though, so get out.
Of your head, stop lying to yourself,
And know the truth.
And it may become tough,

But that's life.
You've got this.
And that is the real truth.

Harley Darlison (13)
The George Eliot Academy, Caldwell

Pretending

"Weirdo, weirdo, weirdo!"
They chanted
"Look at him, *hahaha*
Look at him"
"Nerd, nerd, nerd!"
They chanted
"Look at her, she's reading a book"
"Look at her, she thinks she's so smart"
They chanted
"Look at them, they want all the attention"
"Do you think you can be on stage?"

"Look at them"
The nerd, the weirdo and the theatre kid whispered
"They are so cool, so popular, so mean"
They were perfect
They fitted in
They did what everyone else did
They were the same

Were they, though?
Were they all trying to fit in?
Were they pretending?
Hiding?
Their feelings and personality
Locked away and the key thrown
Do we become robots?

All the same
Just to fit in
To be 'real'

Do we all get labelled?
"Weirdo, nerd, theatre!"
They chanted, they yelled, they screamed

Then the world went
Quiet
"Be real in a fake world"
They whispered the beautiful truth.

Erika Gritco (12)
The George Eliot Academy, Caldwell

A Beautiful Truth

In the shadows deep, where whispers creep,
A teen walks paths, both lost and steep,
With dreams like stars that flicker and fade,
They navigate a world that feels like a charade,

Fingers trace the scars of doubt,
In crowded halls they scream but shout,
A heavy heart
Yearning for a place to start,

Eyes downcast,
The weight of the world,
In laughter's echoes,
Their pains unfurled,
Friendship shifts like grains of sand,
Trust can crumble with a single hand,

Social feeds parade the perfect scene,
While inside they wrestle with what's unseen,
Behind smiles, struggles lie,
A dance with shadows, a fleeting sigh,

Yet, through the storms, resilience grows,
In the quiet moments, a strength grows,
For every year, a lesson learned,
In the fires of youth, their spirits burned,

So, here's to the teens, fierce and true,
Navigating life in shades of blue,
May they find their voice,
Their light to shine, in the harshest moments,
The stars align.

Shannon Brown (11)
The George Eliot Academy, Caldwell

Grey

In life, there is death.
In good, there is evil.
This place hurts even more than a needle.
There are so many people taking their final breath.
Mothers and fathers,
Siblings and partners.
Who knows who'll be next after?

Is the world truly a filthy place?
Or is it fair with love and grace?
There's racism and sexism.
Clouds of grey too.
But don't forget the happiness and peace,
Through and through.

We must ask ourselves,
What really is freedom?
And what does it mean to bring justice?
Our society has been sundered with thunder and blunder.
Some people are forced to be as tough as tungsten.
But they still think they are the weakest among us.

There are secrets and lies,
Why can't we open our eyes to the right size?
It'll be okay though.
We just have to be real in a fake world.

The world isn't all black and white.
It's a combination of grey.
And that's the beautiful truth.

Venissa Thapa (12)
The George Eliot Academy, Caldwell

Be Real In A Fake World

"Be real in a fake world,"
That's what they say,
But it's not that easy.
The constant noise of the judging,
The master of the feelings,
The same thing that goes on and on.

But why?
Why bully all those with pure beauty?
We are all one of a kind.
Don't judge us just because we are different.
Follow the quote which is so underrated.
'Don't judge a book by its cover'.

So next time you name-call a beautiful person,
Think about it,
Do you want them to live with that horrible name,
That has been engraved in their soul?
No, no, no.
It's not okay.
So, call them by their actual name.

Don't follow all the bad things in the world,
Believe in yourself, that's all that matters.

Ignore all the monsters who fill your soul with all the bad things.
Look at yourself and tell yourself every day, you're great.
And look at the world like it's a totally different place.

Jenna Pearce (13)
The George Eliot Academy, Caldwell

Untitled

They call me 'the equestrian', 'the horse girl', and 'the animal kid'
The hurt streams through my head, clouding my eyes and changing the way I see myself
The beautiful truth
Beauty for me is my family, my horses, my cat

My friends call me weird, and it feels like everyone around looks down on me
My emotions start to drown in waves of guilt
Guilt that I freak people out
I am now blinded by the feelings embedded deep inside
My hopes and dreams shatter like glass

A wise woman then told me that the best thing you can be is yourself
Her words touched me, and I knew that I should not let anybody get to me.
I found a new friend with the same hobbies and interests as me
It felt like a massive weight was lifted from my shoulders
I felt like I belonged

Remember that sadness can turn into happiness, just by someone's kind words
Sometimes you just need someone to understand you
The beautiful truth.

Jazmine Brennan (13)
The George Eliot Academy, Caldwell

Games And Getting Out There

I am a gamer and I bet a lot of you are too,
But you should get out there,
Or let someone play with you.
Enjoy the time you and your family have left.
So, hop on the fun express.

There are lots of games out there,
Some are fun but some give you a scare.
All games are fun, but get out there,
Enjoy the sun,
Get known, out in the world.

Games like Minecraft are so creative,
But others are so hated.
Fortnite is so competitive,
But Monopoly is exciting.
Don't always play already-made games.

Your games are the best,
So, bring out your nest.
Your nest is your creativity, so run wild,
Let it be free,
Never back down and just be you.

Ethan Nicholls (12)
The George Eliot Academy, Caldwell

The Duality Of Man

In a world that is harsh and full of danger;
Truth is swarmed with lies
And as reality is drowned in forgery and fame
But when even just one beautiful truth,
Can bring back our hope,
And shine a light on the darkness.

In a world that is kind and full of beauty,
Amazement supported by justice.
And so the nature of reality is shown,
But despite this beauty,
Nothing good is meant to stay.
And darkness drains hope from the lights.

In a world full of destruction and hope,
Death is drenched in solemnity,
Beauty and truth lie hidden.
A balance of light and dark is all that is needed.
Hope and despair,
One cannot exist without another.

Eli Linnett (12)
The George Eliot Academy, Caldwell

Our World

T ogether we live in harmony.
H urting and hunting animals has to stop.
E very living thing deserves a chance.

F ind yourself in the mist.
U nder the bed may be monsters, but ignore them.
T he truth is your best ally.
U m is not a word, it's a sound.
R each for more.
E xcept others.

P lan your life before there's no time.
L ying is your worst enemy.
A nimals will die from pollution.
N ever give up.
E veryone should be safe.
T here is no Planet 'B'.

Adam Hawthorne (12)
The George Eliot Academy, Caldwell

The Beautiful Truth

The beautiful truth.
Is it even there?
The lies and bullying,
That's not the truth.

Skin, hair, religion,
That doesn't matter.
Beauty is everywhere,
And in everyone.

Don't doubt yourself.
You are beautiful.
We are beautiful.
Beauty is the truth and ugliness is an opinion.

They aren't you.
They don't know you.
Not feeling like you're enough and doubting your beauty.
They don't feel your pain.
Your pain is what makes you continue.
Your pain is your beauty.

"The Beautiful Truth."

Kara Hart (12)
The George Eliot Academy, Caldwell

Stars And Raindrops

Look up at the sky,
Stars and raindrops,
Stars and raindrops,
Raindrops shall fall,
Problems be gone,
With stars and raindrops,

The beautiful truth,
Falls with raindrops,
You come to us as
Stars in the sky,
The ones you love are always there,
In the stars and raindrops,
Stars and raindrops,

When you smile,
It may be fake,
Remember you're not
Alone,
Stars and raindrops,
Rise and fall,
Around you,

Never forget the beauty of
Stars and raindrops.

Ria Punjani (12)
The George Eliot Academy, Caldwell

Beautiful Animals

B uzz of bees
E xcitement of others
A mbitious bugs
U nmistakable songs of birds
T ime slows down
I n the garden
F ull of life
U ndeniably serene
L imited never with time

A nd adventures to be made
N ever a dull moment
I n the garden of wonders
M any animals love it
A nd many people do too
L iving in a dream
S urreal views always to be seen.

Evie Meusel (12)
The George Eliot Academy, Caldwell

How To Be Real When The World Is Fake

How to be real when the world is fake
How to live when the world turns to ash
How to speak when the world is in flames
How to sing when the world rots away

How to make sense of the wars and death
How to have friends as fun fades to nothing
How to bury the sadness among the mist

How to learn about nations filled with abominations.
How to hold knowledge of demise with all the misery inside.

Lucas Brookes Salman (13)
The George Eliot Academy, Caldwell

The Beautiful Truth

The truth is my love for my brother, Jacob
He has autism.
I'm more of his big sister than his little sister.

I can't express how much I love him.
Even though he might not show it,
I know he loves me.
I know he really does.

My brother is a pain
But he is a nice guy,
Even though his disabilities
Get in the way sometimes.

I still love him.

Macie Walsh (12)
The George Eliot Academy, Caldwell

Be Real In A Fake World

The beautiful truth
Hidden behind the mask of the face
Craving one thing
The true feeling of a warm embrace

For others, however
The mask fades through
These lucky people's emotions
Thrive in love and truth

Those who lie confined
They crave real emotion
They wish to be hit
With a fantasy potion.

Jamie Wainman (12)
The George Eliot Academy, Caldwell

Untitled

If everyone was the same
Then no one would be different
So, even if you're not the same as someone
You don't have to change
Just be yourself.

Freddie Jones (12)
The George Eliot Academy, Caldwell

The Mask

I grasp the mask to cover the flaws
I hold the self-portrait another hand draws
I play the cards yet to be dealt
Each card unveils a secret I never knew of myself.
A smile stitched tight, as shadows play
I dance through night and call it day
I open the door, but don't walk through
I light the match, but the fire's blue
The fire is peril, but cannot be seen
A flame that flickers where secrets have been
The armour is steel, but I still feel pain
Pain, pain, pain
Beneath its weight, the heart distorts
A trickster, a liar, greedy for more
Truth is a blade, slicing through the night
I stitch it to silence, yet the scars burn bright
Each morning's light, a careful chore
I craft myself, but long for more
A hunger gnaws that cannot be quelled
My sweet tooth aches for the lies I've upheld
It turns to yellow, disguised as gold
Then reveals the black, where shadows unfold
Is there an end to this endless night?
Will the scream's echo never be drowned?
Will my heart remain adrift and never to be found?

Down, down, down, where the shadows reside
But truly there are no shadows in the depths of night.

Esther Amago (13)
Tomlinscote School, Frimley

YOUNG WRITERS INFORMATION

We hope you have enjoyed reading this book – and that you will continue to in the coming years.

If you're the parent or family member of an enthusiastic poet or story writer, do visit our website **www.youngwriters.co.uk/subscribe** and sign up to receive news, competitions, writing challenges and tips, activities and much, much more! There's lots to keep budding writers motivated!

If you would like to order further copies of this book, or any of our other titles, then please give us a call or order via your online account.

Young Writers
Remus House
Coltsfoot Drive
Peterborough
PE2 9BF
(01733) 890066
info@youngwriters.co.uk

Join in the conversation!
Tips, news, giveaways and much more!

YoungWritersUK YoungWritersCW

youngwriterscw youngwriterscw